87$ ЯIOI

# Writing Exercises
# from *Exercise Exchange*

Edited by Littleton Long

D1256783

National Council of Teachers of English
1111 Kenyon Road, Urbana, Illinois 61801

# Writing Exercises from *Exercise Exchange*

# Acknowledgments

Many of these articles, reprinted from *Exercise Exchange*, were reprinted by special permission from the University of Vermont and the University of Connecticut. A large number of articles were reprinted by arrangement with Holt, Rinehart and Winston and Thomas W. Wilcox. Alice Baldwin, author of "New Dimensions in Understanding," graciously granted permission to reprint her article from *The Northfield Schools Bulletin.*

NCTE Editorial Board: Charles R. Cooper, Evelyn M. Copeland, Bernice E. Cullinan, Donald C. Stewart, Frank Zidonis, Robert F. Hogan, *ex officio*, Paul O'Dea, *ex officio.*
Staff Editor: Carol Schanche. Book Design: Rob Carter.

NCTE Stock Number: 59079

© 1976 by the National Council of Teachers of English.
All rights reserved. Printed in the United States of America.

**Library of Congress Cataloging in Publication Data**
Main entry under title:

Writing exercises from Exercise exchange.

   Bibliography: p.
   1.   English language—Rhetoric—Study and teaching (Higher) I.  Long, Littleton.  II.  Exercise exchange.
PE1404.W7    808'.042'0712    76-8014
ISBN 0-8141-5907-9

# Contents

# Foreword

The present collection focuses on writing exercises, both expository and creative, and the areas of adjacent concern from prewriting to rewriting. The editor has necessarily been guided in his selection of the best exercises by what previous editors have chosen to publish; for example, there are no exercises involving argumentation. Clear thinking is generally represented, formal logic is not. I have aimed at assembling the most attractive and usable pieces printed during the last twenty-three years, most of them proving timeless in their application to recurring problems faced in high school and college teaching. While the collection does not purport to be a text or to furnish exercises on every phase of the writing process, there are suggestions in the broad fields of prewriting, diction, paragraphs, style, ideas for themes in general (with specific sections on description, research, and the short story) and concluding material on rewriting techniques.

While most of these exercises were submitted by persons currently teaching on college campuses, many of them had also been used in secondary schools or could be used there successfully. In selecting the material I have been guided by my recent experiences in supervising practice teachers in junior high and high schools. Never having been told that this or that "won't work," these prospective teachers often gave innovative, tough assignments with astonishing success to ninth through twelfth graders. To be sure, these younger students haven't the depth of background reading that enables a college undergraduate to tackle certain problems in literary analysis, but many writing skills seem not too dependent on that sort of sophistication, maturity and experience. Thus I have not tried to separate "high school" exercises and "college" exercises. If there are special problems of class level, the Author's Comment usually brings them out clearly enough. Of the over fifty exercises here presented, then, all but a handful qualify as "general," that is, usable both in high school and in college courses in composition, creative writing, or basic literature.

If there is a kind of universality in the application of these exercises, there is great variety in their substance. Sensitive teachers, alert to the needs and achievements of their own classes, will see that they can modify exercises to fit particular groups or individuals. Indeed, individuality might be said to be the keynote of the pieces in this anthology. Some of them spring from literary foundations, but most are *sui generis*. Eighteen of them, in fact, are short and self-contained enough for that sometimes awkward first class meeting after a vacation. A few were originally designed as tests occupying from fifteen minutes to a whole class period. Others are designed to involve several days' work both in and out of class. And within the nine sections of the Table of Contents, wherever it proved feasible, there is a kind of progression from basic and essential concerns toward the more complex or sophisticated. In sum, while there is great variety among the exercises themselves, two elements unify the collection—a common concern for good training in writing and a common history of practical success in actual classroom use.

# Preface

More than two decades ago Professor Thomas W.Wilcox, then of
Bennington College, had this brilliant idea: Why not make it possible for teachers to share with other teachers those practices,
gimmicks, exercises, assignments, and devices that had proved
useful in their classrooms? How often in the corridor or faculty
lounge have we passed on to others some teaching idea that
worked successfully for us? How often have we appealed to an
older colleague for help in getting through some pedagogical
problem that somehow we couldn't solve on our own? *Exercise
Exchange: A Journal for Teachers of English in High Schools and
Colleges* was conceived, issued forth, and flourished as a medium for circulating classroom successes to aid others in the
profession. Its field of interest included literature, language, media, film, creative writing, composition, and so on. Under Professor Wilcox's editorship for ten years at Bennington, two years
at the University of Alaska, and finally under the sponsorship of
the University of Connecticut, *Exercise Exchange* enabled hundreds of teachers to share their suggestions with thousands of
their colleagues. In its last two years at the University of Connecticut, editorial responsibility was turned over to Professor
Thomas J. Roberts, who was aided in the final issue by Professor
Irving Cummings. Between 1955 and 1968 Holt, Rinehart, and
Winston, publishing the journal free under the editorial care of
Ms. Marie Lonning and Mr. Kenney Withers, built up a mailing list
of eight thousand readers. Since 1972, with initial support from
the College of Arts and Sciences, the journal has been published
by the University of Vermont's Department of English. Professors
Paul A. Eschholz and Alfred F. Rosa were initially editors. Achiev-

ing some years as many as five issues, the journal now appears in October and April. Anyone wishing to submit manuscripts or to subscribe may write to the journal at the Department of English, University of Vermont, Burlington, Vermont 05401.

Special thanks for assistance in this project go to former editors Eschholz and Rosa, and to Arthur W. Biddle (my predecessor as Managing Editor), all of the University of Vermont's Department of English, as well as (fundamentally) to Thomas W. Wilcox.

# Prewriting

Broadly speaking, prewriting includes everything a person has done, learned, felt, or fantasized about up to the moment of writing. Narrowly, it refers to those preparations undertaken for this particular paper on this particular topic—the adoption of a point of view, a tone of voice or attitude toward the material, an approach that will facilitate the writing, and an understanding of the scope or size of the audience to whom the paper is addressed.

# Self-Awareness for Prewriting

John Sweet

*Calling into the conscious mind the students' responses to their environment leads to concrete and specific essays, according to John Sweet of Horace Greeley High School, Chappaqua, New York.*

## Author's Comment

A colleague once declared that the function of English was "to make students more aware of themselves, who they were, and how they related to the world around them." I tried to devise a way of dramatizing this concept to students by directly immersing them in their own sensory and mental skills.

## Assignment

Take a sheet of paper and write at the top, "No one will see these remarks except me." I am going to read aloud to you several directives and questions. Write the answers on your paper.

1   How many colors can you count in your present field of vision?
2   Close your eyes and count the different sounds you can hear. Now open your eyes and listen carefully again. Describe clearly two of those sounds.
3   What might most immediately strike the attention of a stranger sitting in this room?
4   Take careful time to feel your clothing fabric, or a book cover, or some object. Try to put that touch sense response into words.
5   How many feet is it from your seat to the farthest point in the room?
6   Do you notice any odors right now? What are they? Describe them as effectively as you can.
7   What clothing was your mother or brother wearing when you left the house this morning? Describe it.
8   Draw a quick sketch of your front door at home.
9   In what year was President Nixon born?
10   What is the biggest problem faced by your father or mother at this particular time?

2

Take these answers home and study what you have done. Write a composition in which you explore what you have learned about yourself and your particular senses, skills, knowledge. Warning: I am not asking for a teary statement of self-scolding. Finally, at the bottom of your theme include a short statement as to what you think this exercise has to do with the subject "English."

## Preparing to Describe

Mildred Riling

*An interesting blend of subjectivity and objectivity brings great variety to a common subject and leads to profitable comparison of results. Ms. Riling teaches at Southeastern State College, Durant, Oklahoma.*

**Author's Comment**
The purposes of this exercise are to make the student aware of the difference between an artistic description and a statistical report; to show how necessary detailed preliminary thinking is to good writing; and to furnish a plan of procedure when the student begins to write a theme. I have found that this assignment results in a theme which is usually satisfying to the students, most of whom are impressed by what they have been able to write.

The area to be described is the classroom. The classroom is chosen as the subject of the theme because it is at hand, and because it does not seem to be a fitting subject for an artistic description.

*Step 1*    The students are asked to select a *viewpoint* from which they will look at the room in their minds as they describe it. The importance of a definite viewpoint in determining the order of arrangement of descriptive details is discussed. Various viewpoints are suggested by teacher and students. Even such unusual viewpoints as the top step of a ladder outside one of the windows are mentioned as possible points from which to see the room in an original and individual way.

*Step 2*    Selection of a *time of day:* Students are asked to contribute ideas about the difference in the way the room would look at different times of the day: early in the morning; after classes have met in it all day; at midnight on a moonlit night.

*Step 3*   Selection of a *season of year:* Imaginations are stimulated by suggestions about the changes made in the room and its occupants by the different seasons.

*Step 4*   Selection of a *mood, feeling,* or *emotion* to fit the time of day and the season chosen: The mood or feeling will be a unifying factor. By keeping it in mind, the student will reject all details which do not fit it.

*Step 5*   The students make a list of *things seen*, choosing only things which fit the time of day, season, and mood chosen, and only things which can be seen from the viewpoint selected. They are asked to write down the thing which they would probably see first, at the top of their list, and proceed to list sights in a natural seeing order.

*Step 6*   The students make a list of *things heard.* Outside noises may come into the room. If it is a night in October, the noise of students holding a pep rally might be heard, etc.

*Step 7*   The students make a list of *things smelled.* This is usually difficult. Vocabulary for odors, taken from a thesaurus, may be written on the blackboard or mimeographed and passed to the class.

*Step 8*   The students make a list of *things felt physically.*

*Step 9*   The students are asked to write the first sentence of their themes, keeping their viewpoint in mind, and beginning with the sensation they think they will experience first. They are warned not to mention themselves, but to begin to paint a word picture.

# Preparing to Write
# Clear Directions

Margaret K. Onion

*Progression from voiced directions in the classroom to territorial exploration with historical embellishments teaches accuracy and close observation. Ms. Onion teaches at Castleton State College, Castleton, Vermont.*

You might make the following proposal to your class: Do visitors like to explore our town or region? If we could write clear directions for interesting walking or driving tours in this area, might the Chamber of Commerce booth or a local store be willing to offer for sale little booklets or single sheets that we could mimeograph for a few cents apiece?

If the class decides to give it a try, the following activities will provide opportunities for practice and analysis prior to writing directions:

1  Play the game Airport many times, each time stopping to make a class list of specific observable characteristics of good directions. Do not let students settle for glib generalizations about what makes some directions work where others fail, and do not let negative prohibitions pass as analysis.

   The game is played as follows: Form a corridor of chairs or other furniture a generous ten feet long and four feet wide, leaving the ends open. At one end, blindfold a player to be the "plane." Strew the passageway in front of the player with obstacles which can be changed for each game. Station a player to be the "control tower" at the opposite end of the runway. Explain that the plane's transmitting apparatus has failed, but that it can still receive messages. Instruct the control tower to guide the plane safely through the obstacle course by sending voiced instructions which cannot be answered or questioned by the crippled plane. If any part of the plane touches an obstacle or runway fence, the plane has crashed, and the game is over.

2  With a class set of $1.00-size Rand McNally *Interstate Road Atlas*, play the map reading game suggested by James Moffett on page 252 of *A Student-Centered Language Arts*

*Curriculum, K-13* to expand further the list of specific characteristics of good directions. Play the game many times in groups of three students; allow the students to teach each other what they know about map reading; point out map resources only to groups in which nobody discovers a particularly helpful bit of information after several games.

Game is played as follows: Prepare a large number of slips of paper, each containing a page reference to the atlases, the name of the place which will be the starting point, and the name of the destination. Be sure that the names of both starting point and destination appear in the locater key at the edge of the map page. Players should turn their backs on the direction-giver who has drawn one of the slips of paper. The direction-giver tells them the page to use in their atlases, the name of the point of departure, and then gives them directions to follow on their maps. Any data on the maps can be used except the name of the destination. The student giving directions cannot see the other players' faces or hands, and they do not interrupt the directions. When the entire route has been described, the direction-giver announces, "Now you should be at your destination," and asks, "Where are you?"

3 Send students out in pairs within any walking area allowable in building, grounds, or neighborhood. Let them choose a destination and make a plan to reach it by a route which can be covered in a specified time. Ask each team to write a concise, utilitarian set of directions, without map or other drawings and, again, without naming the destination. Exchange directions between teams; set a time limit within which teams should be able to walk to the mystery destinations following each other's written directions; reassemble to compare times, successes, confusions, and further insights into the secrets of good direction giving. By this time it should be clear to the class that giving directions demands extraordinary empathy.

4 Go to professional writings to study tour directions with various focuses of interest. Different parts of the country will have their own resources available to them. Examples from New England might include the Boston *Sunday Globe* "Shunpike" trip descriptions, brochures of Boston's historic walking tours, and *Vermont Life's* "Backroad Tour" articles by Samuel Ogden. Go out in small groups, if supervision can be provided

that way, but let each student be prepared to make observations and notes so as to write tour directions with a specific theme or interest. Exchange and try them out. Reassemble and consider: Did these directions make me feel bright and competent? Did I learn from this tour or notice things I had never noticed before?

When all these practices have been completed at an unhurried pace and with constant analysis of the deep structure of good directions, the class may be ready to do the kind of assignment we often expect too soon. They may find that they really can select some trips with tourist appeal, gather data without wasting mileage, prepare clear, entertaining tour guides worth illustrating, polishing, and offering for sale.

# The Taxonomy of Subject Matter: An Introduction to Outlining

John B. Lord

*The logic behind classification and outlining grows before the students' eyes and leads to a variety of possible theses on the common theme of car safety. Mr. Lord is professor of English at Washington State University, Pullman, Washington.*

## Author's Comment
Most students think of outlining as something which is supposed to be done to a piece of writing after somebody else has written it, rather than as a means of preparing a paper. I use this exercise as an introduction to the second (and I think only proper) use of the outline. The exercise is done by conference, without any special assignments having been prepared in anticipation, for, say, the first class after a vacation.

Announce that the class is to prepare a paper on the subject of "The Causes of Automobile Accidents" (or on any other suitable subject). Starting at some point in the class and proceeding throughout the class until the well runs dry, ask each student to name some cause of automobile accidents—anything from icy roads to drunken drivers. As each suggestion is advanced, write it on the board. Do not attempt to classify in any way, but simply put the suggestions down in the order given. If someone says "Car in need of repair," and the next one says, "Faulty steering shaft," put them both down. You'll need them later. If, however, someone offers an exact duplicate of a previous entry, it may properly be thrown into synonymy.

After ten or fifteen minutes you will have a sizeable, but unsorted, mass of causes, and almost certainly a few protesting students who have seen the overlapping and duplication of categories. If you lack such students, it is easy to prod with questions until you find some, and you proceed to the next stage, classification as to species and genus.

In another fifteen minutes, it is usually easy to persuade the class to divide the list into three main groups: causes arising in the driver, causes arising in the car, and causes arising in road conditions. These last will further be subdivided into such categories as the road proper, the weather, the time of day or night, and comparative crowdedness of traffic.

This is usually as far as I care to take a class before starting on the final stage, although further subclassification can obviously be done.

The final stage is the study of the organized data in an attempt to discover a plausible thesis. Examples:

*Simple:*       There are three main causes of automobile accidents—the car, the road, and the driver.

*Compound:* Manufacturers have for years been improving (or have recently begun to improve) the safety of our cars; engineers have greatly improved our roads; it's about time someone started doing something about our drivers.

*Complex:*     Although manufacturers claim to be making safer cars and engineers to be constructing safer roads, the limitations of human physical and mental capacities actually result in more danger than ever.

And so forth, ad lib.

**Summary**
The main point of this exercise is that until the students have organized this mass of material, and reflected on the significance of the formal categories which they have uncovered, they are unable to observe any intrinsic, implicit thesis or to plan a coherent, unified, amply developed paper expounding it.

# Pertinence in the Outline

Henry A. Person

*This exercise brings out the difference between supporting an idea or thesis and merely dealing with the same general subject matter. Mr. Person submitted this exercise while at the University of Washington, Seattle, Washington.*

**Author's Comment**
This exercise emphasizes and clarifies the relations between subtopics and main topics in the outline, and between developing sentences and topic sentence in the paragraph. In addition, it makes clear the logical reason for subordination within the sentence and the reason for avoiding excessive coordination.

In the exercise, all the numbered sentences are *on* the subject indicated by the governing sentence, but not all of them are pertinent; i.e., they do not *prove, illustrate,* or *corroborate* the governing statement. Some of them need to be deleted entirely; others need restatement. Occasionally matters can be remedied by rephrasing the governing statement, e.g. to correct upside-down subordination.

The numbered statements are intended to prove, illustrate, or substantiate the governing statements above them. Some of them do and some of them do not.

Point out which statements fail to satisfy the requirements of unity and pertinence, and explain why they are at fault. Indicate whether the faulty statements call for revision or for deletion. Remember, it is not a question of whether they are true; but of whether they are pertinent *as stated.*

I  A lake in the mountains is the best place for a vacation.
1  The fishing is good.
2  One can enjoy such water sports as boating and swimming.
3  There are shady woods to hike in.
4  At such a lake one can enjoy bonfires in the evening.

II  Dancing is an excellent form of recreation.
1  To be able to dance well is an accomplishment.
2  Dancing helps to rest one's mind.
3  Dancing teaches one to be a good mixer among strangers.

III  The average sorority has a bad influence on most of its active members.
1  Girls love to show off their fine clothes.
2  Many girls are boy-crazy.
3  Social activities are placed above studying.
4  Health is neglected.

IV  There are fewer sicknesses now than there were a century ago.
1  Cities are more sanitary.
2  We know more about the human body.
3  We have learned more about various medicines.
4  There are more doctors and hospitals nowadays.
5  Polio is almost conquered.

V  It is great fun to spear dogfish at night from a small boat.
1  The dogfish belongs to the shark family.
2  It has a three-chambered heart.
3  You must have a quick, skillful oarsman at the oars.

VI  Our presidents have come from many walks of life.
1  George Washington was our first president and he was a surveyor and a plantation owner.
2  President Grant was once a storekeeper.
3  Lincoln, who was a lawyer, was president during the Civil War.
4  Woodrow Wilson was a college president.

VII  Spring fever has bad effects on most college students.
1  The warm, sunny days produce a contagious laziness.

2  Spring fever hinders or prevents one's studying
   adequately.
3  Students come to college primarily for an education.
4  It is very pleasant to go canoeing in the early spring.

VIII  Smoking is a disgusting and detrimental habit.
   1  Smoking causes or aggravates a number of ailments.
   2  The he-man cigar ads on TV are pretty silly.
   3  Smokers may be seen at any time or place.
   4  If a person does not smoke, he or she is considered
      a poor sport.

IX  Slum conditions cause juvenile delinquency.
   1  Slum-district houses are rundown and obsolete.
   2  Children grow up in crowded, unwholesome conditions.
   3  There are no open fields or large parks.
   4  Young people crave action and excitement.
   5  Children from broken homes often end up in court.

X  The corner saloon offers its patrons varied entertainment.
   1  The corner saloon is an old institution.
   2  Friends meet there regularly on the way home from
      work.
   3  Many "regulars" go there every day.
   4  In some taverns there is musical entertainment.
   5  The sporting customers can play shuffleboard.
   6  Those with gambling instincts can play the punch
      boards.

XI  Television is not a complete blessing.
   1  The set costs a lot of money.
   2  I don't care for Johnny Carson.
   3  Many of the movies are 30 years old.
   4  The wrestling matches are all fakes.

XII  Functionally, the modern car is an absurdity.
   1  Its length and width make it hard to park.
   2  With room for seven people it usually hauls one person.
   3  It has more power than it needs.
   4  Two-tone paint jobs are just a passing fad.
   5  Foreign cars have air-cooled engines.

## Further Comments

I The numbered sentences, however true, are all nonpertinent, since none of them proves or helps to prove the governing statement. Nothing but comparison with others could prove that a place is *best.* One could remedy matters formally by changing *best* to *good.*

II Number 1 is true, but irrelevant; 2 and 3 are pertinent.

III All are nonpertinent, since none are connected with sororities. In 3 and 4 the trouble is caused by passive construction.

IV All are nonpertinent, since the governing statement requires quantitative comparative proof. After the proof is given, the numbered sentences could be used to explain how this condition came about. They would fit under some such statement as: *Several factors help to account for the decrease in illness during the past century.*

V All are nonpertinent.

VI Numbers 2 and 4 are acceptable as they stand; 1 has faultily coordinated statements; 3 has upside-down subordination.

VII Numbers 1 and 2 are okay; 3 and 4 are faulty.

VIII Number 1 is okay; 2, 3, and 4 are faulty.

IX All faulty; not tied up with delinquency.

X Numbers 1, 2, and 3 are faulty; they belong under a different governing statement. Numbers 4, 5, and 6 are okay.

XI Governing statement is bad because it is a negation. It is very difficult to prove something is *not.* Number 2 is completely irrelevant; the others need restating unless the governing sentence itself is changed.

XII Numbers 1, 2, and 3 are okay; 4 and 5 are faulty but could be cured by rephrasing.

[Not all teachers will agree with the definition of "pertinence" revealed in the answers supplied here. Tom Wilcox]

# A Checklist to Improve Writing Papers

Lynn Z. Bloom and
Rebecca S. Wild

*Searching questions help students clarify their topic, support it, orga-nize it, avoid mechanical errors, and enhance stylistic effectiveness* before *the final version. Ms. Bloom now teaches at the University of New Mexico, Albuquerque, New Mexico, and Ms. Wild is at Eastern Illinois University, Charleston, Illinois.*

## Author's Comment

We distribute the "Check List" to students at the beginning of the course so they may refer to it when writing their own themes and when evaluating the themes of others. We also use it as the basis of our own theme grading, and tell our students so. This furnishes the students with a fairly explicit list of our own criteria for evaluating student papers, and it keeps our grading from becoming as subjective and occult as it might otherwise get. The Check List may appropriately accompany any grammar handbook the teacher selects.

## Check List

I Topic
   A Is the exact point you wish to make clear to you? Is there an exact point? Have you framed this accurately and concisely in your thesis? Does your thesis cover the whole subject of your essay?
   B Have you used any words in your thesis which can be misconstrued or which defy precise definition?

II Issues
   A Have you limited your topic sufficiently so that it can be thoroughly and accurately treated in your paper?
   B Within limits you've established, have you exhausted possibilities of discussion? Have you considered your topic from the relevant political, economic, religious, social, intellectual, and aesthetic angles? or others?
   C Will reference to laws or rules help proof? (Divine, moral, governmental, sociological, psychological?) Will reference to customs, tastes, techniques help?

D   Will reference to experience help proof? (History, folklore, maxims? Own personal observation? Hearsay, and authoritativeness of the informant?)

III  Organization

  A  Beginning

    1  Is the problem isolated and limited immediately?

    2  Is your stand firm and definite?

    3  Are any definitions needed?

    4  Can anything be omitted without doing violence to your viewpoint?

  B  Middle

    1  What is your strongest point? Where is it?

    2  Have you slid over or ignored important points?

    3  Where are the minor points (if any) mentioned in your paper?

    4  What will the opposition counter to each of your points? Have you built an answer into each discussion?

    5  Does paragraphing help definition of your points?

    6  Is there a pattern for the arrangement of the points? Do you have legitimate reasons for such a pattern?

    7  Check for false generalities, missing steps, non-sequitur conclusions. Check also for insufficient illustrations, inadequate documentation, failure to acknowledge and account for exceptions.

  C  End

    1  Does the ending follow easily and necessarily from your strongest point(s) and from all the points? Or could your reader have stopped short of this?

    2  Is there a fresh observation to add interest? A forceful tying together of all the aspects presented? Does the tone of your conclusion fit the tone of your paper?

IV  Mechanics

  A  Grammar

Recheck grammar book for understanding of previous errors and then search paper for like mistakes. When in doubt about mechanics, check appropriate handbook section.

B   Diction

Check up-to-date collegiate dictionary definition of any word not perfectly common or natural to you. Does the added weight in meaning or novelty compensate for the danger of seeming affected or pompous? Does the word fit your paper generally in respect to sense, general tone, topic, and intended audience? Check dictionary for spelling, for division at line end.

V   Style

A   What level(s) of language are you using? Are these appropriate to your intended audience? to your approach to the subject? Have you included colloquialisms inappropriate to the level of language used?

B   What is your tone? Is it consistent? Is it appropriate, both to subject and to audience?

C   If you have used metaphors and other imagery, dialogue, personification, characterization, or vivid descriptive writing:

  1   Do they enhance or detract from your presentation of the subject?

  2   Are they appropriate and relevant to the presentation of the subject?

  3   If you haven't used them, should you?

D   What is the ratio of figurative to literal speech in your paper?

Now, are you satisfied with your paper? If not, are you willing to do something to remedy this dissatisfaction *before* you hand in the paper?

# Diction

The seamless garment of successful composition blends choice of words, figures of speech, attitude, tone, organization, etc. into a single whole of interdependent parts. Nevertheless, the basic material is words—right words, colorful words, accurate, fresh, harmonizing words.

# How Do You Define "Ceiling"?

Walker Gibson

*The importance of viewpoint in intercommunication comes out clearly here. Walker Gibson now teaches English at the University of Massachusetts, Amherst, Massachusetts.*

"Ceiling" is defined in Air Force weather manuals as that level at which the sky is more than half covered by clouds. At night this level can be "measured" by the following process. A searchlight is trained directly upward, perpendicular to the earth. Another searchlight, at a known distance from the first light, is trained to cross the first light's beam at the point where the lowest perceptible bank of clouds is illuminated. A simple protractor device is used to determine the angle of the second beam with respect to the earth's surface. In this manner two angles and the base of a right triangle are "known," and by use of the Pythagorean theorem the altitude of the triangle can be quickly found. This figure is entered as the "ceiling."

One starless, windy night a weather observer at an Army air base carefully went through this process. The figure he reached was 550. He telephoned the radio tower at the base and told the operator there, *"The ceiling is now 550 feet."*

A half hour later a plane a few miles away called in to the tower and requested weather information at this field. The tower man gave it to the pilot, and in a few minutes the plane landed. Half a minute later the pilot burst into the weather office.

"You're crazy!" he said to the weather observer. *"The ceiling is only 300.* I didn't see a thing till I was practically on the ground. Don't you know you can kill people that way?"

"Yes sir," said the weather observer.

1 Think about the meaning of "ceiling" in the context of the weather observer's statement to the tower operator.
2 Think about the meaning of "ceiling" in the context of the pilot's statement to the weather observer.

3   Suppose you were the commanding general of the base where this event occurred. What might you do to prevent such things from happening? What experts might you call in to advise you? (The answer to that one is a good rhetorician!) Write a memorandum to the troops in which you provide them with information or advice calculated to prevent the recurrence of events like this one.

# Fictionary in the Classroom

William A. Stephany

*Imagination and imitation of dictionary style and method combine here with the fun of tricking one's classmates. Mr. Stephany is at the University of Vermont, Burlington, Vermont.*

Near the end of last semester, I excused my expository writing class from other assignments so they could devote their time to their final papers. I wanted to do something, however, to keep people coming to class, so I could continue to speak about the final papers and help them solve any individual problems they might have been running into while working on them. I hit upon the idea, therefore, of adapting the old party game, Fictionary, to class use. The game is familiar, no doubt, under a variety of names, and ground rules are probably not identical in all locales. The essential rule of the game, though, is that participants make up plausible sounding definitions for obscure words in an effort to coax other players into guessing that theirs is the real dictionary definition.

This is the procedure that I followed in class. On Monday I wrote on the board four obscure words and asked the class to write their bluffed definitions by Wednesday. (Such words can be found on virtually every page of an unabridged dictionary.) I added the request that anyone who might by chance know the real meaning of a word write a bluff definition so there would only be one "right" answer. On Wednesday I collected their definitions. On Friday I handed out a dittoed list of their definitions, printed in no particular order, adding to the list the real definition, and I asked each person in the class to select the most reasonable sounding definition for each word. The usual way to keep score in Fictionary is to award one point each time a player guesses the real definition and one point to the player who made up the bluff each time another player guesses incorrectly. Although my class showed little interest in determining a winner, another class might very well decide that this would be appropriate.

The class was unanimous in thinking the game was fun, worth playing with future classes, and a useful and worthwhile part of a writing class. Although their conclusions seemed disparate, they really boiled down to just two. One was that the exercise reminded them of the uses of a dictionary. If they wanted to make their definitions truly persuasive, they had to rediscover the kinds of information a dictionary entry supplies. Definitions were inherently more persuasive, they found, if they included etymologies, indications of the date at which the word supposedly entered the language, specialized vocabulary, if any, pronunciation, multiple definitions, and the like. Secondly, they realized the extreme efficiency required in writing a dictionary entry. In trying to emulate this, they learned something about controlling words and excising those that are irrelevant.

My own conclusion is related to theirs: the game involves a useful miniaturization of the whole writing process. It takes imagination and wit to come up with a plausible idea and precise wording to make the idea persuasive. Mimicking the style of a dictionary carries with it the value of any disciplined act of imitation, with the advantage that students eagerly take part in the imitation when the end is the fairly immediate one of fooling their friends. The exercise also places a premium on such stylistic niceties as diction and tone, two points which it is often difficult to make concrete and visible. Finally, my students found it extremely difficult to write thoroughly believable entries spontaneously. It was the final fussing with detail, the final fussing after the "last" draft was completed, that usually spelled the difference between a clever attempt and a truly persuasive and successful achievement. Both of these, of course, are factors common to good writing in general.

I will conclude with some examples from my students' work. The following two definitions of "scruto" are instructive for the way in which they fall just short of being really persuasive. One of them, "A fine brush used in archaeological digging to remove fine particles of soil," would work but for the repetition of the adjective "fine." The second, which includes part of speech and etymological source, is even more persuasive: "*n.* [Latin] Ancient brush-like writing tool used by monks to copy the Bible." Except that "ancient" is vague and not likely to be used to cover some indeterminate period in the Middle Ages, this is reasonable sounding. I will conclude with several definitions that are well crafted, striking the right tone and including the right amount of appropriate detail.

scruto, *n.* The inner curtain which divides the audience from the stage in a proscenium theatre.

prodromus, *n.* A hard woody shell covering the soft fleshy buds of certain shrubs (e.g. pussy willows). Shell is shed in early spring when bud begins to develop.

caliche. A small musical instrument that gained some popularity in Southern Europe in the early 18th century; it was similar to a harpsichord, but smaller, and had a poorer tone quality.

caliche, *n.* Stiff lacy neck piece worn by men during Victorian era.

The exercise was very successful with an advanced composition class, but would probably be easily adapted to almost any English class in junior high school or higher, and would probably make as natural an addition to a unit on the dictionary as it did to a writing class.

# Close Reading for Clear Writing (I)

Jeffrey Fleece

*The following two exercises stress the practical need for clarity in diction and sentence structure in laws—as in all areas of communication. Mr. Fleece is at the University of Hawaii, Honolulu, Hawaii.*

## Author's Comment

Change-of-pace exercises like the following (others can be made up from the income-tax instructions) help students recognize the importance of accurate statement and the pleasure of playing with language problems. For a welcome novelty, men seem to enjoy this kind of exercise more than women, and do better with it. Allow about 15 minutes; don't take the grades very seriously.

> **Read the following law (which contains a loophole) and answer the questions.**
>
> Section 4854, Revised Statutes of Missouri (Habitual Criminal Act)—If any person convicted of any offense punishable by imprisonment in the penitentiary or of any attempt to commit an offense which, if perpetrated, would be punishable by imprisonment in the penitentiary, shall be discharged either upon pardon or upon compliance with the sentence, and shall subsequently be convicted of any offense committed after such pardon or discharge, he shall be punished as follows: any legal punishment shall be increased by 25%.

1  What is the subject (or subjects) and what is the verb (or verbs) of the clause that begins with "If" at the beginning of the sentence?
2  Joe Doques, who once spent the night in jail on a charge of disturbing the peace after a drunken spree, is convicted of a careless driving charge for which the normal maximum legal sentence is four months. He is sentenced to the penitentiary for five months. Is this legal? Why?
3  Willie Harris spent six months in the penitentiary for unarmed robbery, the minimum legal sentence. He commits the same felony again and is again given the same sentence. Is this legal? Why?
4  The maximum punishment for unarmed robbery is two years.

Would it be legal for Willie Harris to be sentenced to the penitentiary for one year for his second offense? Why?

5    Jack Cade, who once committed armed assault and was in the penitentiary thirteen years out of a fifteen-year sentence, was tried for a new felony while out on parole (definition of parole—"a conditional release of a prisoner with an unexpired sentence"). This time he was convicted of a felony for which he could normally be sent to the penitentiary for from one to eight years. He was sentenced to a new term of ten years, his parole was revoked, and he was returned to the penitentiary for twelve years. Was this legal? Why?

*Note: The loophole, that the law may not be applied to parolees, has actually been tested in court.* The answers are these: 2 is not legal because a jail is not a penitentiary; 3 is not legal because "shall be increased" means "must be increased"; 4 is legal, a legal sentence of 4/5 of a year plus 25%; 5 is not legal. Jack Cade had not been pardoned nor had he served out his first sentence before committing the second offense; he was a parolee and thus exempt from this law.

# Close Reading for Clear Writing (II)

D. L. Emblen

*Mr. Emblen contributed this "linguistic tangle," as he called it, from Santa Rosa Junior College, Santa Rosa, California.*

### Author's Comment

As an introduction to a series of reading and composition problems, the following exercise has proved useful, early in the semester, in stimulating students to pursue clarity in composition.

1    The following passage, taken verbatim from Section 13833 California Education Code, is dictated to the students:

> Where the governing board arranges to pay persons employed by it in 12 equal installments for the year, and, in the event any such person dies during the school year, that

salary paid the decedent prior to his death subtracted from the amount equal to that portion of his annual salary as bears the same ratio to the established annual salary for his position as the number of days of the school year (as defined in the Education Code Section 8101) during which he was employed prior to his death bears to the total number of days of the school year.

2   Students are asked to study the passage and answer the following questions:
     a   Is the passage a complete sentence?
     b   What is the simple subject and simple predicate?
     c   What does the passage say?
        (To assist students in answering this question, the following problem is given):

> An instructor is hired at $10,000 per year.
> He works 45 days of the 180-day school year.
> He dies.
> He has received four monthly checks.
> How much is his widow entitled to?

3   Students are required to rewrite the passage and submit it, along with the answers to the questions, at the next class meeting.
4   Completed exercise serves as a springboard for a discussion of clarity, with particular reference to sentence structure.

# Finding Exact Meanings

S. B. Wynburne

*This tricky exercise will test both reading ability and a student's sense of how a paragraph should develop. Mr. Wynburne contributes from Stranmillis Teachers' Training College, Belfast, Northern Ireland.*

Give the EXACT MEANING of the following passage in about 100 words:

> The England of Shakespeare and Bacon was still largely mediaeval in its economic organization and social outlook, more interested in maintaining customary standards of con-

sumption than in accumulating capital for future production, with an aristocracy contemptuous of the economic virtues, a peasantry farming for subsistence amid the organized confusion of the open-field village, and a small, if growing, body of jealously conservative craftsmen. In such a society Puritanism worked like the yeast which sets the whole mass fermenting. It went through its slack and loosely knit texture like a troop of Cromwell's Ironsides through the disorderly cavalry of Rupert. The English of about 1600 did their business as it had been done in 800 and their views on society had changed little from that time. They were more interested in keeping up the normal level of drink, food, and clothes than in storing money to produce goods for the future. The men of high birth looked down their noses at those who were full of care for money and goods. The purpose of the farmers was to get enough, but not more, from their fields which were placed in order round their groups of houses but, in fact, mixed up and so hard to get to. As well, the small but increasing group of men whose work was shaping wood, iron, and stone hated competition and kept out outsiders. In a nation with a loosely joined framework of this sort, the Protestant outlook, based on complete belief in the Bible, had a quick, strong effect on everyone. (258 words)

**Author's Comment**
The above is an examination (or class) question that can be set to test the reading ability of students. The passage consists of 100 words from Tawney's *Religion and the Rise of Capitalism* followed immediately, and without a break, by a sense version (paraphrase) in simplified English. Half an hour would allow ample time for the students to meditate (a) on the meaning of the words "exact meaning" in the direction, and (b) to discover that the first 100 words include the sense of the lines that follow them. Anyone who either copies out the first 100 words or indicates clearly that the answer is the first part of the passage down to the words ". . . of Rupert" should get full marks. Out of 277 eighteen- to nineteen-year-old candidate teachers who had to tackle a very similar question, only 17 got full marks. Obviously the element of surprise in this type of question is essential: any sort of warning would rob it of all its limited and *ad hoc* value. The student who, with half an hour to work, has failed to see the relationship between the two sections will, on recovering from rage and shame, be more open to exhortations on the need to read carefully. In

class, a scrutiny of the differences between the "meaning" and the "sense" would show that logic (cf. I. A. Richards) is an examination of translations and a complete process of definition.

# Invigorating Vocabulary Building

Harry P. Kroitor

*Though it starts at the chalkboard, this device easily turns into a homework assignment that guides the writing and rewriting of themes toward concreteness, exactness, and vividness. Mr. Kroitor teaches at Texas A & M University, College Station, Texas.*

## Author's Comment
Here's an exercise designed to show students that they have an untapped vocabulary potential, that concreteness and variety in writing may be achieved with intelligent effort. The exercise can be introduced at various points in the students' English growth: when connotation and denotation are studied, when vocabulary building is stressed (antonyms, synonyms), when rewriting vague sentences is required. For the instructor, the exercise is a tool readily adaptable to the problems of diction study; to the student it suggests one road to self-improvement in a difficult area. Best results come when two or three consecutive class periods are devoted to the work.

## Exercise I: Oral
1   Write on the board a simple sentence, preferably one that is vague. Example: "A man went into the building."
2   Ask the class to study each word in turn and then to suggest synonyms, antonyms, or other equivalents that will make the original word more concrete and expressive.
3   Using the class suggestions, write below each word in the original sentence the substitution given. For example, by directing class attention to the indefinite article, *a*, and by suggesting at the same time that it functions as an adjective, the instructor should soon receive equivalents like *one, the, the old (young, short, tall, thin, emaciated)*. By a similar proc-

ess the word *man* can become *drunkard, critic, cynic, optimist, pessimist, philanthropist, criminal, businessman* (exclude the professionals).

4   The finished product on the board might look something like this:

| A | man | went | into the building. |
|---|-----|------|--------------------|
| One | drunkard | staggered | tavern |
| The | critic | ran | house |
| The old | cynic | crept | edifice |
| The young | optimist | sneaked | hut |
| The tall | pessimist | walked | shed |
| The short | criminal | slipped | shack |
| The thin | | crawled | |
| The fat | | stumbled | |

5   Ask a mathematician in the class to work out the number of variations possible: this creates interest and surprise.

**Exercise II: Follow Through**
A   Select carefully three simple sentences for the students to work on at home, using the method outlined above. Sentences should be selected to explore the students' recognition vocabulary in several distinctive areas: poetry, science, engineering, astronomy, education, philosophy, church, law. The instructor may control the exercise by restricting (or expanding) the students' word choice, thus exploring areas of strength or weakness.

B   When students have written their themes, the follow-through becomes most important and most practical. While marking a set of themes, underline clearly one vague sentence (or more) in each student theme; then ask the students to apply the method outlined above to explore their vocabulary for more concrete, suggestive words. Although the subject of their themes will necessarily limit the vocabulary from which they may draw, they still should be able to devise at least six good variations for the original sentence.

# Making New Metaphors

Howard C. Brashers

*Encouraging freshness both avoids cliché writing and exercises students' taste in determining what metaphors suit the larger intentions of an essay or story. Mr. Brashers's exercise comes from San Diego State University, San Diego, California.*

## Author's Comment

This exercise was used originally in a college creative writing class, but I have since used it profitably with high school students and in both regular composition and creative writing classes. This exercise helps students to begin thinking in metaphorical terms and gives them a method with which they can deliberately create new images for specific, preconceived thematic purposes. The method makes novelty and insight manipulable. Some of this material appeared in a rather different form, addressed to a different audience, in the author's *Creative Writing: Fiction, Drama, Poetry, and the Essay,* (American Book Co., 1968).

It is a philosophical curiosity that the truly original would be impossible to conceive, so we typically explain newness as realignments of the old. Thus our Martians, moon-men, and other monsters all have eyes, since we cannot imagine a being without sensory perceptors; and they have feet, or wings, or move by levitation, since we cannot conceive of them moving except by means we are already familiar with. True, we may translate them, transmogrify them, trans-substantiate them, trans-materialize them —but these methods, too, we are already familiar with, though we may not be able to explain them. Once enough familiar elements are combined in ways they have never before been combined, we have novelty. Novelty generally passes for originality, in literature and life.

By deliberately juxtaposing unlike items, we can create novel images, similes, metaphors, and other figures of speech. By deliberately choosing the sources of the items to be juxtaposed, we can control the thematic implications that the figures of speech will communicate.

**Preparation for the Exercise**
The teacher will need to approach the exercise with some inductive discussion, in order to give the student a clear idea of what is expected. One might begin, for example, by considering with the students what elements are combined in such a common cliché as "wind-swept waves." It may well have been consciously, deliberately created. It must have been originated by a housewife or husband who noticed that dust fogs out before a broom in waves, then went to the beach and noticed that the wind pushes the water into similar configurations. What a stroke of originality that must have been, when fresh! Of course, it is also quite easy, the kind of thing almost anyone would think of—like looking at the stars and thinking of human insignificance. In literature, we usually demand that the writer look harder for comparisons, and part of our aesthetic response is to the difficulty.

The teacher may also wish to point out that it was this kind of aesthetic response to activities of the mind that Dr. Johnson was talking about when he described wit as novel combination of the familiar. "Wit," said Johnson in his famous criticism of metaphysical poetry, ". . . may be more rigorously and philosophically considered as a kind of *discordia concors*; a combination of dissimilar images, or discovery of occult resemblances in things apparently unlike . . . the most heterogeneous ideas . . . yoked by violence together." The joining may be bizarre or bland, but the most important thing for the writer to realize is that it may be done, and done consciously. The conscious impulse toward novel wit is what produces both our literary works, those "discoveries" about ourselves, and our clichés, those prefabricated henhouses of unthinking minds.

**The Exercise and a Sample**
At its best, the exercise goes through four stages: first, the student goes to some place, any place, say the living room of his or her own home, and writes down twenty-five nouns, verbs, or adjectives that the place brings to mind. Second, the student goes to some quite different place, say the beach, and writes down twenty-five other nouns, verbs, adjectives. Third, the student combines words or concepts from the two lists to make original images or metaphors. One comes up with a certain burden of

wind-swept waves, people as thick as flies or packed like sardines, of course, but one may also come up with a rug of sand, a curtain of rock, a man gasping like a grunion, tide-pools of sentimental souls, or something even novel, witty, or original. Fourth, the students write a paragraph, or a familiar essay, or a poem, using the matrix of metaphors and other images they have discovered.

It is important to keep the students aware that, by choosing the sources of their images, they can deliberately produce a particular, preconceived effect. Let's say one of them wants to write a satire about a variety store. The student goes to such a store and writes down the dozen or twenty-five words that will best evoke the image and type of the variety store. Then he or she goes to a source of negative, dirty, derogatory imagery, let's say a junk yard or a second-hand furniture store. The student may get lists like these:

| *Variety Store* | *Junk Shop* |
|---|---|
| sleepy cashier | cobwebs |
| toothbrushes | crud |
| clocks | dust |
| nylon scarves | paint flecking off |
| manikins | out-dated furniture |
| keys | old-fashioned |
| toys | crystal glassware |
| gaudy colors, red, | silver, tarnished |
|    yellow, blue | dog-eared books |
| cheap glasses | spilled paint |
| thimbles and thread | fly-specks |
| polished wood | "dust-kittens" on floor |
| mirrors | |
| brass lamps | |

It is obvious that some of these words are unusable. Words like *crud, clocks, furniture* are too slangy, too merely nominal, or too general for use in any very novel perception. And it is also obvious that certain combinations of prior experience take place in the making of the lists: the transfer of the polished quality of manikins and wooden counters to customers; the dust-kittens on the floor. Such combinations themselves become material for further combinations.

Using the two lists above, a writer might come up with something like this:

> The old-fashioned sofa of a girl behind the fly-speck of a cash register gazed with cobweb eyes at polished manikins; sold dog-eared scarves, tarnished toothbrushes, and spilled-paint mirrors to gaudy, polished, dust-kitten customers with thimble and thread minds.

### Follow-Ups to the Exercise

There are three important things to remind the student of as the exercise is nearing completion or is being repeated with new lists: first, taste and critical evaluation must operate on every new combination. The example above illustrates the variety of result that one can get via deliberate combination of two lists. "Old-fashioned sofa of a girl" strikes me as a bit cute, though it is also quite evocative. I suppose we've all known girls who, draped in chintz, would be comfortable to sit on. "Fly-speck of a cash register" seems to be begging. It asks me to associate the negative connotations of "fly-speck," not the fly-speck itself, with the cash register. This seems dangerous. It begs for a response that is not entirely on the page, but has to come out of a stock response to fly-specks. "Cobweb eyes" seems to me quite good. Excellent. It evokes the dry, static, hazy quality one sees in the eyes of the benighted, and I even see the veins in an eye, crystalized like the radiating threads of a web. "Polished manikins" is dead. It evokes only what everyone would take to be a part of the definition of *manikin.* "Dog-eared scarves" is fair-to-good. It merely applies clichéd perception to a new object. Such a figure will do to "swell a progress," undercut before an excellence, contribute to a scene—but it is not strong enough to carry the core of a poem or story. "Tarnished toothbrushes" is bad, ba-a-a-d. In this day of plastics, it is impossible, ergo the begging. The attempt to save the figure with alliteration only calls attention to the feebleness of the attempt. "Spilled-paint mirrors" comes off after a bit of thought. First, turn it into a simile: mirrors like spilled paint. Then, enumerate the qualities: wavy surface, bubbles at the edges, irregular, accidental in design, rather than precisely engineered, cheap, tawdry. It does its duty, but not so immediately as "cobweb eyes." "Gaudy, polished, dust-kitten customers" suffers from more than one fault: gaudy and dust contradict; so do polished and dust; dust-kitten may be a bit eso-teric or regional; there is begging all the way. But the most ser-ious fault, it seems to me, is the figure's adjectivitis. Piling up of adjectives is no way to evoke a clear image. "Thimble and thread minds" is somewhere between being cute and doing duty after thought. The writer who would deliberately combine lists must also exercise taste and critical ability. One excellent image out of a list is one image ahead.

Second, the results may seem so meager as to make the device unprofitable, but don't blanch before you have considered some of the great literature that seems to have sprung from this very process. Our whole conception of the conceit and of the matrix of metaphor is nothing more nor less than deliberate combina-tions of lists. Shakespeare must have been quite conscious and calculating when he sat down to describe the Renaissance con-ventions of the rejected lover in the terminology of the bank-ruptcy court: "When to the sessions of sweet silent thought . . . ." And he even tells us of his deliberation in "Shall I compare thee to a summer's day. . . ." He reverses the process with nega-tive, or false, comparisons in "My mistress' eyes are nothing like the sun. . . ." All through our literary history, we can find myriad examples where a conscious writer has not settled for the one or two images from a list, but has gone on to force combination af-ter combination into novel insight.

Third, as Mark Schorer has pointed out in his essay, "Fiction and the 'Analogical Matrix,' " the thematic implications of this kind of strategy are very important. "Metaphorical language expresses, defines, and evaluates theme, and thereby demonstrates the limits and the special poise within those limits of a given imag-ination." The careful, conscious, and thoughtful writer—in other words, the serious writer—will be greatly concerned with the im-plications of this over-simplified mental gymnastic, for its mechanism is the same at the highest level of creative achieve-ment as here. It is a means by which the poise, limits, and mean-ings of a writer's perceptions can be made manifest. It is a way in which writers eliminate accident and control communication.

# Recognizing Prefabricated Phrasing

Patrick E. Kilburn

*Utilizing stale phrases, empty locutions, and inefficient sentence forms can help students avoid them in serious work. Mr. Kilburn teaches at Union College, Schenectady, New York.*

## Author's Comment

One should avoid excessive solemnity about composition. The following exercise can enliven a dull period and help to sensitize students to mushy verbiage by requiring them to use padding deliberately, which also carries with it a minor thrill of the forbidden, since they write, under the sanction of the teacher, as wordily as they can. There is, of course, nothing sacred about the quoted paragraph; any tightly knit, well-written passage will do.

## Directions

With practice, an imaginative student can take an almost unlimited number of words to say next to nothing. Around a mere nubbin of thought and without straining a brain cell or adding an iota of meaning, one can erect a huge warehouse of prefabricated phrases that looks entirely substantial to all eyes except those of the cynical. The following exercise will help you to develop this valuable skill. The paragraph is from Jacques Barzun's *Teacher in America* (Anchor, 1955), p. 17. With the aid of the list of prefabricated phrases and all-purpose words below, and others which will readily occur to you, see how big and substantial-looking a building you can erect around Barzun's paragraph without losing the idea completely.

> All the knowledge, skill, art, and science that we use and revere, up to Einstein's formulas about the stars, is a mere repetition and extension of the initial feat of learning to walk. But this extension does not take place by itself. Most of it has to be taught, slowly and painfully. There was a time when Mr. Einstein was not quite sure what eight times nine came to. He had to learn, and to learn he had to be taught. The reason teaching has to go on is that children are not born human; they are made so. The wretched foundlings that were occasionally discovered in rural parts of Europe a hundred years ago walked on all fours and grunted like beasts.

**Prefabricated Phrases**

The basic fundamental truth is that . . .

The truth remains that . . .

The answer is that . . .

I believe that (or in my opinion) . . .

I would not hesitate to agree that . . .

This brings us to the essence of the question of . . .

Let me clarify the statement that . . .

However, there remains the fact that . . .

It is quite possible (or doubtful) that . . .

All this proves the theory that . . .

I would like to prove my point by saying that . . .

I would like to say, here and now, that . . .

I would like to cite a good example to the effect that . . .

It is clear that . . .

It may be pointed out that . . .

One could almost (or easily) believe that . . .

One might almost say that . . .

The truth of this assertion could very easily be demon-
strated by saying that . . .

The conclusion is that . . .

We need to realize (or it must be realized) that . . .

This can all be summed up by saying that . . .

To illustrate my point of view, let me say that . . .

**All-Purpose Sentence Modifiers**

as a whole, in this situation, in such a case, in my opinion, in general, in the last analysis, sooner or later, now and then, to the people in our modern society of the space age, in our modern day and age, to a certain extent (or degree), more importantly

**All-Purpose Phrases to Be Used before Nouns**

the same as, so-called, what might almost be called, what is essentially equivalent (or comparable) to, hardly more than, very much (or almost exactly) like, could hardly (or almost) be said to be

**Especially Useful Words**

factor, category, type

**Especially Useful Constructions**
There is . . . which (or who), it is . . . which (or who). Use this in conjunction with the passive voice. Thus, never say, "John threw the ball," but always, "It was the ball which was thrown by John."

# Affective vs. Informative Diction

Barbara LeBost

*This series of exercises lets students practice fitting two basic kinds of diction to appropriate subjects, organization, and audiences. Ms. LeBost submitted this exercise from Oakland City College, Oakland, California.*

**Author's Comment**
The following exercises might be used in a brief (three to seven weeks) unit on language. The purpose of a short, four-week unit in a freshman composition course is to heighten students' understanding of language and how it operates in order that they may use clear principles of writing in their own work. Two chapters from S. I. Hayakawa's *Language in Thought and Action* are read as the basis for further observation and writing. "The Language of Affective Communication" and "Giving Things Names" discuss the problems of classification, information, expressive and poetic language, levels of writing, and so on.

**Exercise: Psychological and Logical Uses of Language**
The first part is devoted to observation and discussion of the language of advertising and political speeches. Students bring in the material and the group as a whole comments on the techniques of persuasion. The affective aspects of language are developed through analysis of the intention of the writers, discussion of the images and symbols used, observation of the purpose and expected results of the material in question. Cigarette ads are perfect for discussion purposes; automobile ads are also interesting. Students soon become quite adept at separating informative from affective language. They also begin to be concerned with the *audience* which various writers are trying to reach. One class became so sophisticated in the process that they noticed

in my lectures on the language of automobile ads I had neglected to discuss any ads for foreign cars. (I own a foreign car.) We soon began comparing the differences between ads for American and foreign cars and found some fascinating uses of language.

Some of Richard Nixon's and Adlai Stevenson's speeches also work well. It is interesting to compare some of the propaganda literature from other countries to contemporary political speeches.

The second part of the unit is an attempt to make these newly discovered writing techniques concrete. Students write every day for two weeks. They are then asked to submit rewritten ads in which they have transformed affective into informative language. Various exercises are added, such as writing two paragraphs, one in slang, the other in formal English, or one organized and the other disorganized; or two paragraphs which express the same idea but are written in jargon, and/or technical language in contrast to the language, for example, of sports or of the jazz musician. These short exercises stress the idea of appropriateness of language, the purpose, and the audience.

The next step in making concrete the ideas we have just discussed is to attempt to explain a game to a foreigner. Many students described the game of baseball, others selected football. This exercise helps them to see that giving a clear description takes precision, economy of language, and a developed sense of the order and arrangement in things. The final exercises in the unit were again centered on giving clear information to the reader with a minimum of affective language. (I should probably note here that affective language, as such, was not considered "bad"; in fact, it was stressed that the emotional effects of much literature depended on the use of affective language.) The purpose here was only to be able to express oneself clearly with brevity and precision. Students were asked to give directions from the college to their houses without the use of diagrams, to explain briefly how to tie one's shoelaces, and to discuss a dance step.

The value of this type of exercise is that students usually will become more aware of the problems of writing in general, and usually will attempt to approach future writing assignments with a fresh view, to leave unfounded generalization behind them, and to use judgment based on reason and fact. After this unit, students can more easily see their own faults in writing. It has been made clear to them that language has many uses and purposes, and that in expository writing it is important that the psychology of language, purpose, audience, and desired effect be taken into consideration.

# Synonymy and Tone

Thomas W. Wilcox

*Appearing in the first issue of* Exercise Exchange, *this group of exercises by the founder of the journal tests students' responses to subtleties of diction and word order. The final portion suggests how far the study of language has come in a century. Mr. Wilcox is now at the University of Connecticut, Storrs, Connecticut.*

**Author's Comment**
In the Language and Literature course we state: "The first purpose of this course is to teach students to understand the nature of language; the second purpose is to acquaint them with language in its literary form."

These exercises were designed to provoke discussion, on a very elementary level, of the problem of synonymy and to encourage students to distinguish variations in tone among apparently synonymous statements. The questions we were trying to answer were: "What happens when you change the words, grammatical structure, or syntactical pattern of a sentence?" and "How can we identify an author's manner of addressing an audience?" The first assignment was designed to be deceptively simple: "Write the same sentence in five different ways." The sentences reprinted below were submitted in response to this assignment. I added the last two groups to illustrate mixed tone and to test their ability to perceive synonymity (or analogy). In each case we began our analysis of the sentence by asking, "What question or questions might this statement answer?" Our purpose was to define meaning in operational terms.

A 1    Jane has loads of pep and energy.
    2    Jane is a very lively girl.
    3    Jane has plenty of vim and vigor.
    4    Jane is a rambunctious child.
    5    Jane is a little live wire.

    1    I am so hungry.
    2    I hope we eat soon.
    3    My stomach is gurgling.
    4    I could eat a horse.
    5    I am dying for something to eat.

    1    I am so thirsty that I am going to get some water.
    2    I'm going to get some water because I'm thirsty.
    3    I'm thirsty and I'm going to get a drink of water.
    4    I'm on my way to get a drink of water because I'm thirsty.
    5    I'm thirsty and I'm leaving to get a drink of water.

    1    Complete relaxation can only be obtained by sleep.
    2    Sleep is the best way to become completely relaxed.
    3    The only way to become completely relaxed is to go to
         sleep.
    4    Some people say that the best way to relax is to lie down
         and try to go to sleep.
    5    Lying down can make one relaxed, but sleep is better.

    1    The peak of Bear Mountain is illuminated by the
         silvery effervescence of the moon.
    2    Each moonlit night, Bear Mountain's summit thrives
         in the moon's beauty.
    3    Moonlight's effect on Bear Mountain is a breath-taking
         spectacle.
    4    The shimmering peak of Bear Mountain seems to quiver
         as it rises majestically in the path of moonlight.
    5    Have you ever seen the phosphorescent crest of Bear
         Mountain when moonbeams shower their light on it?

    1    Joan awakened at seven o'clock, and she went down-
         stairs to breakfast.
    2    Since it was already seven o'clock when Joan awakened,
         she jumped out of bed and ran downstairs to breakfast.
    3    Joan knew that breakfast was always at seven o'clock,
         so she hurried out of bed and downstairs.
    4    "Oh, my goodness! It's seven o'clock. I must hurry
         downstairs for breakfast," Joan said upon awakening.

5 When Joan awakened at seven o'clock, the thought of breakfast increased her speed downstairs.

1 Personnel will refrain from discussing classified matter.
2 Don't tell our secrets.
3 Don't be a tattle-tale.
4 Keep mum.
5 Personnel will keep mum.

1 Stone walls do not a prison make, nor iron bars a cage.
2 Freedom is the recognition of necessity.
3 In His will is our peace.

B 1 Write *two* paraphrases of the following passage:

> Abstention from labor is not only a honorific or meritorious act, but it presently comes to be a requisite of decency. The insistence on property as the basis of reputability is very naive and very imperious during the early stages of the accumulation of wealth. Abstention from labor is the conventional evidence of wealth and is therefore the conventional mark of social standing; and this instance of the meritoriousness of wealth leads to a more strenuous insistence on leisure. According to well-established laws of human nature, prescription presently seizes upon this conventional evidence of wealth and fixes it in men's habits of thought as something that is in itself substantially meritorious and ennobling; while productive labor at the same time and by a like process becomes in a double sense intrinsically unworthy. Prescription ends by making labor not only disreputable in the eyes of the community, but morally impossible to the noble freeborn man, and incompatible with a worthy life.
>
> **From Veblen's *Theory of the Leisure Class***
> (This information was not given to the students.)

2 Write four parallel sentences, each one uniform in tone, using one of the following nouns in each: "female," "lady," "dame," and "woman."

3 Choosing wisely among the synonyms for uniform tone, make three sentences out of the following:

He 
{ smelled / experienced / breathed in } 
a 
{ lousy / bad / fetid } 
{ olfactory sensation. / stink. / odor. }

4  In the light of what you have learned in performing these exercises, discuss the theory of language implicit in the following passage:

It is to those who are painfully groping their way and struggling with the difficulties of composition that this work professes to hold out a helping hand. The assistance it gives is that of furnishing on every topic a copious store of words and phrases, adapted to express all the recognizable shades and modifications of the general idea under which those words and phrases are arranged. The inquirer can readily select, out of the ample collection spread before his eyes in the following pages, those expressions which are best suited to his purpose, and which might not have occurred to him without such assistance. In order to make this selection, he scarcely ever need engage in any critical or elaborate study of the subtle distinctions existing between synonymous terms; for if the materials set before him be sufficiently abundant, an instinctive tact will rarely fail to lead him to the proper choice. Even while glancing over the columns of this work, his eye may chance to light upon a particular term which may save the cost of a clumsy paraphrase, or spare the labor of a tortuous circumlocution. Some felicitous turn of expression thus introduced will frequently open to the mind of the reader a whole vista of collateral ideas, which could not, without an extended and obtrusive episode, have been unfolded to his view; and often will the judicious insertion of a happy epithet, like a beam of sunshine in a landscape, illumine and adorn the subject which it touches, imparting new grace and giving life and spirit to the picture.

**From the Introduction to Roget's *Thesaurus*.**

5  Compare Roget's point of view with C. O. Sylvester Mawson's "A Word of Caution" prefacing his "dictionary form" edition of Roget's *Thesaurus*. [Littleton Long]

# Theme, Thesis, and Paragraph

The heart of the writing experience, according to many experts on composition, is the thesis and its development through the topic sentence and the organic paragraph (invented, English teachers are always surprised to learn, only in the middle of the nineteenth century). All of the exercises here lend themselves to reworking with other material in a wide variety of levels and applications, and all give practice in relating ideas to their proofs or illustrations and in separating big ideas from smaller ones.

# Stating a Thesis Precisely

Lauren A. King

*Writing an essay without clarifying the thesis guarantees fuzziness, irrelevance, and frustration for the reader. Mr. King, now retired, sent this assignment from Malone College, Canton, Ohio.*

Many students have difficulty in understanding what is involved in the clarification of a thesis in exposition. Moreover, they often fall short of a complete clarification of general statements in the body of a paper. By the presentation of a theory and a method of clarification, this exercise is intended to aid the student in understanding the importance of clarification and in avoiding underdeveloped statements. The theory is that the thesis includes certain "dark spots," usually actual words, demanding explanation, and that these spots are clarified by more specific and detailed statements, which in turn have their own "dark spots." Thus a process of clarification is set up, which must be continued until all spots have been clarified in the detail desirable for the particular writing situation at hand.

An example will show the theory in practice. Here is a sentence which could serve as a thesis for papers of varying length: "New York had a strong mayor who was an honest professional 'municipal manager' and who ran a completely 'good' city government." Discussion will find three "dark spots" in this thesis: (1) "strong" in this context, (2) "professional 'municipal manager,' " and (3) "good" in this context and obviously special meaning indicated by the punctuation.

Further discussion will perhaps develop the idea that "strong" can mean strong as related either to the extent of the powers exercised or to the manner of exercising them, or both. Here then is the idea that begins to clarify "strong," but requires in turn further clarification. Suppose the writer intends to indicate that "strong" refers to the manner of administering the office. What makes a "strong" mayor in this sense? Discussion will elicit a list of qualities of strength: decisiveness, fairness, honesty, loyalty to employees, search for competent subordinates. If these

42

phrases are made sufficiently specific and concrete, perhaps this original "dark spot" has been clarified. However, a question of how this spot might be still further clarified into a sort of super-clarity will lead to the use of examples of behavior having the specified quality. Such elaborate development would be desirable in a long paper, but not in a short one, of course.

The other two "dark spots" can be discussed in the same manner.

This method, if persisted in, will develop habits of careful and full exposition of a thesis, as well as of general statements in the body of a paper. Sometimes it is desirable to require an accompanying commentary explaining the process followed and decisions made.

# Theme and Thesis

John B. Lord

*Whether in literary criticism or exposition, the theme (subject area) must be distinguished from the thesis (an arguable idea about the subject matter). Mr. Lord submits exercises from Washington State University, Pullman, Washington.*

**Author's Comment**
This exercise will serve in any course in which students write papers which argue a point. The illustration below comes from a survey course. Because the *Beowulf* is the first work which students read in this particular course, I use that poem to make the point of this exercise. Obviously I could use any literary work or any field of discourse to make the same point: that a theme, and a thesis about that theme, are two very distinct ideas. Until students have grasped the distinction, they will continue to write papers which, while they may reassure the instructor that the student has read the work under discussion, will not persuade him or her that the student has thought about the work, or changed in any way as a result of having read it.

I assign a series of short papers, each of which must isolate a theme (i.e., a true subject) from the work read thus far, must restrict that theme to suitable size, and must present some arguable thesis about it—an assignment so very generally given in any classroom that many teachers assume that all students know what a thesis is and how it differs from a theme. I submit that the assumption is unjustified, and have devised this exercise to clarify the distinction.

**Exercise**

1  Suppose that you choose for your theme, "The Religious Motif in the *Beowulf*." What assertions can you make about that theme?
    a  Religion is very important in that poem.
    b  The religion is monotheistic. (Maybe. Wyrd? Metod? etc.? All same God?)
    c  The religion is Christian. (Maybe. Sole identifying reference is to Cain and Abel. What other religions might the reference identify? How do you eliminate them?)
    d  The Christianity of *Beowulf* is more Old Testament than New Testament in its general tone.
    e  (Let's stop here; we've gone just far enough.)

2  How does the last assertion differ from the first? More or less discussion, depending on the class, will serve to bring out the ideas that:
    a  The first assertion states a truth so obvious in the poem itself that a reader will learn it better by reading the poem than by reading the paper which argues the point.
    b  By contrast the last statement must be derived from evidence in the poem which must then be compared with evidence drawn from elsewhere, so that the asserted conclusion is not explicit in the poem, but implicit.
    c  The same difference is to be found between each of the steps, though to a lesser degree.

3  The reason why a paper which argued point 1a above ("Religion is very important in the *Beowulf*") would be a poor paper is that the writer would make no contribution to the reader which the reader could not find better in the poem itself. But the paper which argues point 1d may be (if otherwise well written) an excellent paper, for it suggests an idea which might not have occurred to the reader at all, and which helps in the understanding of the poem. Themes are explicit; theses implicit.

# Analyzing Paragraph Structure

Donald H. Cunningham

*Though sometimes given other names, two kinds of sentences besides the topic sentence must be distinguished if the writer is to produce paragraphs that develop adequately. Mr. Cunningham sent this exercise from Southern Illinois University, Carbondale, Illinois.*

Paragraph construction used by many writers consists of three basic types of sentences (according to their function in a paragraph): topic sentences, explanatory sentences, and exemplification sentences. These may appear in any order in a paragraph but primarily in the order listed. Of the three types of sentences there may be more than one, especially of the explanatory and exemplification sentences.

A number of paragraphs from my classes' reading material illustrate this development of paragraphs. The following paragraph has only a topic sentence and exemplification sentences:

> Today the changes taking place in Afghanistan are sweeping, impressive, and sometimes, in their cold war context, alarming. The bootless Afghan soldier who once earned Pakistani contempt for his slovenly appearance and homemade gun at the Khyber Pass now drives a Soviet T54 tank or cuts vapor swaths in a MIG-19 above the Hindu Kush. Women have discarded the *borqa.* Oil is gushing from new wells in the northeast. Glass, briquette, fruit-processing, textile, and fertilizer plants are in production. Fine new highways, already built or under construction, are linking the main towns and burrowing through the mountains.
> **—"The Atlantic Report: Afghanistan"**
> *The Atlantic Monthly,* **(October, 1962) 29.**

A paragraph from Gilbert Highet's *Talents and Geniuses* uses all three types of sentences:

> Sir Winston Churchill's six-volume work *The Second World War* is really an autobiographical record. He himself says it is "the Story as I knew and experienced it as Prime Minister and Minister of Defence of Great Britain." Therefore it cannot be called anything like a complete history of the war. For example, Churchill tells the story of one of the crucial events of

the war, one of the crucial events of this century—the reduction of Japan to impotence and surrender by intensive bombardment culminating in what he calls the "casting" of two atomic bombs—in only eight pages, while a greater amount of wordage is devoted to a reprint of the broadcast which he made to British listeners on VE day.

Using this paragraph or similar ones, I ask my students to reconstruct the paragraph in the following manner: place the topic sentence against the normal left margin of the page and type it in all capital letters; place the explanatory sentence on an imaginary margin five spaces in from the normal left margin of the page and underline it. Place the exemplification sentences on an imaginary margin ten spaces in from the normal left margin of the page. Each sentence, then, regardless of where it occurs in a paragraph, begins at its appropriate margin, designating graphically, according to function, which type of sentence it is. For example, Highet's paragraph has the following three-marginal profile:

| | |
|---|---|
| SIR WINSTON CHURCHILL'S SIX-VOLUME WORK *THE SECOND WORLD WAR* IS REALLY AN AUTOBIOGRAPHICAL RECORD. | Topic Sentence |
| *He himself says it is "the Story as I knew and experienced it as Prime Minister and Minister of Defence of Great Britain."* | Explanatory Sentence |
| *Therefore it cannot be called anything like a completed history of the war.* | Explanatory Sentence |
| For example, Churchill tells the story of one of the curcial events of the war, one of the crucial events of this century—the reduction of Japan to impotence and surrender by intensive bombardment culminating in what he calls the "casting" of two atomic bombs—in only eight pages, while a greater amount of wordage is devoted to a reprint of the broadcast which he made to British listeners on VE day. | Exemplification Sentence |

Assignment: Have your students analyze the following paragraph from Clyde Kluckhohn's *Mirror for Man* by placing the sentences on their appropriate margin.

> From the anthropological point of view there are as many different worlds upon the earth as there are languages. Each language is an instrument which guides people in observing, in reacting, in expressing themselves in a special way. The pie of experience can be sliced in many different ways, and language is the principal directive force in the background. You can't say in Chinese, "answer me yes or no." Chinese gives priority to "how?" and nonexclusive categories. In English we have both real plurals and imaginary plurals, "ten men" and "ten days"; in Hopi plurals and cardinal numbers may be used only for things that can be seen together as an objective group. The fundamental categories of the French verb are before and after (tense) and potentiality vs. actuality (mood); the fundamental categories of one American Indian language (Wintu) are subjectivity vs. objectivity, knowledge vs. belief, freedom vs. actual necessity.

After observing this basic paragraph pattern, have each student begin a similar program of paragraphing by completing a number of assignments suitable for paragraph topics. The three-marginal profile shown above is used during composition as an aid for the student in constructing his or her paragraph and checking the development of topic sentences. You can use it to check the developmental paragraphs of their essays.

# Coherence in the Paragraph

James Stronks

*Paragraph unity and coherence are subtly tested in the next exercise, contributed by James Stronks from the University of Illinois at Chicago Circle, Chicago, Illinois.*

**Author's Comment**
This exercise is designed to force students to examine a paragraph's organization more closely than ever before, with the object of becoming fully aware of such features as movement, coherence, continuity, and unity. The exercise may be mimeographed on 8½x14-inch paper, then cut in half at the dotted line, the top half to be distributed when the assignment is made, the bottom half to be handed out at the next meeting, after the discussion has reached the right stage for the "official solution." See "Further Comment," below.

**The Problem**
The following sentences have been scrambled into incorrect order, but when correctly rearranged they form a coherent paragraph. Taken from a book about Mark Twain, the paragraph is a comparison of Twain and Lincoln. To make it more interesting, an extraneous sentence has been mixed in, one which does not belong in the paragraph. The paragraph is complete in itself; it makes perfect sense standing alone, and it is not closely related to the previous paragraph. *Directions:* (1) Cut the sentences free from each other. (2) Clue: Find what appears to be the topic sentence and put it first. (3) Paying attention to the transitions, arrange the sentences into their most logical order and throw out the one which does not belong. If there seem to be several sentences which could go in any order, closer study will discover a logical sequence even for them. (4) When the sentences are correctly rearranged, paste them on a sheet of paper and bring the paragraph to class. (5) In class you will be given the paragraph as it was originally written. Be prepared to defend your version of it, as well as your deletion of a particular sentence. Here are the scrambled sentences:

1   Both were deeply acquainted with melancholy and despair; both were fatalists.
2   As humorists, both felt the basic gravity of humor; with both it was an adaptation of the mind, a reflex of the struggle to be sane; both knew, and Mark Twain said, that there is no humor in heaven.
3   Both spent their boyhoods in a society that was still essentially frontier; both were rivermen.
4   There are striking affinities between Lincoln and Mark Twain.
5   It was of such resemblances that William Dean Howells was thinking when he called Mark Twain "the Lincoln of our literature."
6   Both absorbed the midcontinental heritage: fiercely equalitarian democracy, hatred of injustice and oppression, the man-to-man individualism of an expanding society.
7   If Lincoln had written novels, he would, without a doubt, have been a greater novelist than Twain.
8   On the other hand, both instinctively used the humor of the common life, and from their earliest years made fables of it.

(Instructor cuts sheet here, hands out bottom part on day of discussion.)

. . . . . . . . . . . . . . . . . . . . . . . . . . . . . . . . . . . . . . . . . . . . . . . . . . .

Here is the paragraph as originally written in Bernard DeVoto's *The Portable Mark Twain* (Viking Press), p. 5. Italics indicate transitional words:

1   (Topic sentence) *There are striking affinities between Lincoln and Mark Twain.*
2   *Both* spent their boyhoods in a society that was still essentially frontier; *both* were rivermen.
3   *Both* absorbed the midcontinental heritage: fiercely equalitarian democracy, hatred of injustice and oppression, the man-to-man individualism of an expanding society.
4   *Both* were deeply acquainted with melancholy and despair; *both* were fatalists.
5   *On the other hand,* both instinctively used the humor of the common life, and from their earliest years made fables of it.

6  *As humorists,* both felt the basic gravity of humor; with both it was an adaptation of the mind, a reflex of the struggle to be sane; both knew, and Mark Twain said, that there is no humor in heaven.

7  *It was of such resemblances* that William Dean Howells was thinking when he called Mark Twain "the Lincoln of our literature."

(The extraneous sentence, No. 7 in the scrambled version, is from an article by William Van O'Connor in *College English,* October, 1955.)

## Further Comment

Although any suitable paragraph in the class textbook may be discussed profitably, the fact that it is frozen in print makes it unwieldy for experimental rearrangement. It is hard to juggle sentences in the head. Hence the value of this dismembered paragraph. When doing this assignment alone, the student's effort to discover the paragraph's most logical organization will prepare him or her well for the postmortem in class the next day and make the student receptive to the conclusions the instructor draws at the end.

The exercises need take only about twenty minutes of discussion, or (hopefully) wrangling, depending on the amount of intelligent stubbornness encountered. The correct version probably should not be sprung until the students have supplied the right reasons for the right sequence (or most of it), but before the subject has been overlabored. If, when the right version is handed out, some argue against its organization, so much the better; that is the kind of hard-eyed and independent attitude hoped for. At some point the instructor will probably want to concede good-naturedly that the "correct" version is not necessarily inevitable. Instructors, having themselves labored over recalcitrant paragraphs in their own writing, may also be willing to grant that there is *sometimes* the possibility of several different, equally good, arrangements for a given paragraph—an admission which students find reassuring, and which they recognize as honest and realistic. The instructor might conclude with the comment that the discussion has emphasized some worthwhile principles, and that it would be pleasant to see them illustrated in the students' next theme.

Important: The instructor should also perform the assignment precisely as the students are asked to do it. This will give his or her management of the exercise an invaluable humility and practicality.

# Three Cures for "Paragraph Paralysis"

Norma J. Engberg

*Enigmatic paragraphs, impromptu paragraphs (where students criticize the teacher's version as well as their own), and two-version paragraphs take some of the drudgery out of learning paragraph techniques. Ms. Engberg teaches at the University of Nevada, Las Vegas, Nevada.*

Every composition instructor, whether at the high school or college level, wants students to do some impromptu writing in the classroom. Often this writing takes the form of a paragraph a page or so in length, and the instructor assigns the topic(s) on the spot. It is immediately obvious, however, that the students have written paragraphs until they are sick of them; boredom, resentment, and the conviction that the teacher never reads the paragraphs anyway—that they are assigned merely as busywork—create a kind of "paragraph paralysis" which the instructor is hard put to combat.

The instructor first must get the students' attention, and one of the best ways of doing this is to surprise them. If I desire a sample of each student's writing the first day of class, I ask the students to write a paragraph at the first of the period on the somewhat enigmatic topic, "What it means if the sky isn't blue," but I do not collect the papers. During the last fifteen minutes I ask for another paragraph, "The most curious thing in my pocket(book)." At the end of the period I let the student decide which of the two he or she wants to hand in. I have aroused the students' curiosity because I have given them a choice.

On another occasion after we have talked about descriptive writing, I bring a rock with a fossil in it to class and pass it around. After recording the rock's weight and dimensions on the board for easy reference, I ask the students to write an imaginative, descriptive, or analytical paragraph taking the rock as their subject.

Several class meetings later, after we have talked about paragraph structure and the principles of revision, I ditto two of the students' "rock" paragraphs and hand them out, instructing the class to correct and revise, writing on the dittoed sheets. After fifteen or twenty minutes, we talk about the students' revisions, and I pass out my own rewritings of these same student paragraphs. Soon the students are criticizing my versions as well as their own. At the end of the session, I collect the dittoed sheets and give them to the two students whose paragraphs were the original subjects of study. Since the students all wrote on the same subject—the fossil rock—earlier, they have an insider's feel of the writer's problems and can revise more intelligently than if they were dealing with some subject drawn from "general knowledge." Furthermore, the students see that different revisions are equally possible and equally correct. They will understand me the next time I tell them that the wordings I note down in the margins of their essays are only suggestions. While singular subjects must be used with singular verbs, word choice and sentence structure are matters of choice, and there is no one right answer.

Some weeks later I open class by asking the students to write a paragraph defining "liberal education" and have the students hold onto their papers as we discuss the day's reading assignment. Toward the end of the period, I ask the students to rewrite, making a new version which is better than or at least different from the first one. The students find themselves saying the same thing in two different ways and choosing one over the other with some basis for this choice. I collect and read both versions of the experiment.

Throughout the semester as I try out these devices, I follow three rules which I set myself from the beginning: I pull such tricks infrequently enough to keep them a surprise; I always read, mark (*not* grade!), and return every paragraph submitted; and I assume the pose of a fellow writer, not of a teacher. By these means I catch and hold the students' attention. As the students themselves have told me, they are able for the first time to read their own writing with some idea of how to revise it. Also, the give-and-take of such cooperative projects, ones in which students and teacher appear to be working together toward a common goal, makes learning to write seem less like the drudgery it is. When students can begin to feel that the hard work of revision is personally rewarding, their improvement is rapid, their grades rise, and they can take justifiable pride in the prose of their accomplishments.

# Style

Beyond correctness and clarity and orderliness, students should be reaching toward control of style—that complicated subject with many overlapping elements—and may be helped by exercises that focus on one or another aspect of the large topic.

# Ceremonial Language Style

Thomas W. Wilcox

*The stability of ceremonial language undergoes investigation here on emotional and intellectual grounds, to demonstrate something about the informative and affective dimensions of public language. Thomas W. Wilcox now teaches at the University of Connecticut, Storrs, Connecticut.*

### Hypothetical Case to Be Considered
A young teacher in an elementary school, Ms. B., noticed that as her pupils recited the "Pledge of Allegiance" each morning, their attention often wandered and they sometimes garbled the text. She correctly surmised from this that the language of the Pledge (e.g., such words as "indivisible") was incomprehensible to her students. Accordingly, she wrote a new version—the most accurate paraphrase or translation she could contrive—so that their daily recitation might have more meaning for her students and thus encourage patriotism among them.

### Directions for Your Paper
1   Write out the traditional version of "I Pledge Allegiance to the Flag."
2   Now write the paraphrase which well-intentioned Ms. B. might have asked her young pupils to commit to memory. That is, write a version of the Pledge better suited to her pupils' understanding.
3   Now write an essay in which you speculate, in logical and well-composed prose, on this question: What would happen to such a public school teacher as the result of her altering the Pledge—and *why* would it happen? What would the community's response to her action be? What would parents, local officers, veterans' organizations, and other spokesmen of communal attitudes say? Why would they respond as you suppose? (And you might ponder this question: What side would *you* take if a controversy about Ms. B.'s action arose?)
4   The final questions to be considered in your essay—and, for our purposes, the most important—are these: What does the community's probable response to Ms. B's reform tell us

about ceremonial uses of language? Is it true that society always respects clarity of language and effectiveness of communication? In what ways, other than by a direct communication of intended meaning, may language affect a communal group? Many other possibilities may be suggested by questions such as these.

## Additional Leads

A  Do you suppose that Ms. B.'s pupils—who we will assume had memorized the traditional Pledge at an earlier age, in an earlier grade—would have approved her altering the verbal ceremony they performed at the beginning of each day's work? What meaning *might* the recitation of the Pledge have had for them?

B  On p. 103 of Leonard F. Dean & Kenneth G. Wilson (*Essays on Language and Usage,* First Edition) you will find a transcript of the Lord's Prayer as it was written in English in the tenth century. Even without knowing much about Old English, you can see that the basic form of this prayer has changed very little in over a thousand years. How can this fact be related to the probable fate of Ms. B. and to attitudes toward language that the community's response to her experiment may have revealed?

# Effective Sentence Style

Seymour Lainoff

*Sentence form, diction, and imagery are shown balancing objectivity and subjectivity to make effective prose. Mr. Lainoff sent this exercise from Yeshiva College, New York, New York.*

## Author's Comment

The following passage is effective (even in translation) because of the balance it maintains between subjectivity and objectivity. A personal experience gives up a general value, a definition; or, conversely, an abstract idea is rendered dramatically, is given the warmth and color of a gradual personal discovery. Throughout the passage, mind and sentiment are intimately united; at any point, one cannot tell where thought ends and feeling begins. The author's chief means in the evolving of his final idea are, first, different sentence structure forms, and, second, imagery. Both sentence structure and image reflect each phase in this evolution.

## Exercise

(1) Looking down on those swarming highways I understood more clearly than ever what peace meant. (2) In time of peace the world is self-contained. (3) The villagers come home at dusk from their fields. (4) The grain is stored up in the barns. (5) The folded linen is piled up in the cupboards. (6) In time of peace each thing is in its place, easily found. (7) Each friend is where he belongs, easily reached. (8) All men know where they will sleep when night comes. (9) Ah, but peace dies when the framework is ripped apart. (10) When there is no longer a place that is yours in the world. (11) When you know no longer where your friend is to be found. (12) Peace is present when man can see the face that is composed of things that have meaning and are in their place. (13) Peace is present when things form part of a whole greater than their sum, as the divers minerals in the ground collect to become the tree.
(14) But this is war.
(15) I can see from my plane the long swarming highways. . . .

**From *Flight to Arras*, by Antoine de Saint Exupéry, translated by Lewis Galantière (Reynal & Hitchcock, 1942).**

1   What do you suppose the author sees from his plane? How do you infer this?
2   Why, from the second through the eighth sentence, does the author use short simple declarative sentences? What is the dominant characteristic of the images of these sentences? What is the effect of the repetitive and parallel structures? (These sentences and images suggest containment, routine, order.)
3   What purpose is served in making the tenth and eleventh sentences fragmentary subordinate clauses? (The fragmented sentences suggest disorder, fragmented relationships.)
4   How does the ninth sentence serve as a transition?
5   By what steps does the author's final definition of peace evolve? (First, by viewing the world at peace; and then by contrasting that world with the world at war. A true definition of peace cannot be learned without a knowledge of both worlds.)

How is the author's final definition more complete than the preliminary definition? Is this completeness mirrored in the sentence structure?
6  What is the effect of the last two (the twelfth and thirteenth) loose sentences in the paragraph? Of the images in these sentences?

# Increasing Awareness of Style

Elisabeth Van Schaack

*Double translation (whose survival Roger Ascham would have applauded) serves to test the superiority of the original. Ms. Van Schaack teaches at the Washburn University of Topeka, Topeka, Kansas.*

This assignment is designed to show the importance of very small details of phrasing and diction. Paragraph 2 is the first paragraph of Katherine Mansfield's story "At the Bay." Paragraph 1 is my translation back into English from a French translation, without reference to the original. The students, not told which is which, are asked to read the two, decide which is the original and therefore better, and defend their choice. Most choose correctly, and the evidence offered emphasizes the point that minute changes in style make a significant difference.

1  In the morning very early. The sun had not yet risen, and the whole bay was hidden by a white fog which had come from the sea. The big brush-covered hills in the background were drowned. One could not see where they ended, or where the meadows and bungalows began. The sandy road had disappeared, along with the bungalows and pastures on the other side; beyond them, there were no more white dunes clothed in reddish grass; there was no sign of a beach, or of the sea. A heavy dew had fallen. The grass was blue. Big drops hung from the bushes, ready to fall but never falling; in the gardens the dampness bent the ranunculuses and the pinks almost to the ground. The cold fuchsias were soaked; round pearls of dew rested on the leaves of the nasturtiums. It was as if the sea had come gently beating up to here in the dark, as

if an immense single wave had come lapping, lapping, up to where? Perhaps, if one had wakened in the night, one would have been able to see a big fish quickly brushing the window and then disappearing.

2 Very early morning. The sun was not yet risen, and the whole of Crescent Bay was hidden under a white sea-mist. The big bush-covered hills at the back were smothered. You could not see where they ended and the paddocks and bungalows began. The sandy road was gone and the paddocks and bungalows the other side of it; there were no white dunes covered with reddish grass beyond them; there was nothing to mark which was beach and where was the sea. A heavy dew had fallen. The grass was blue. Big drops hung on the bushes and just did not fall; all the marigolds and the pinks in the bungalow gardens were bowed to the earth with wetness. Drenched were the cold fuchsias, round pearls of dew lay on the flat nasturtium leaves. It looked as though the sea had beaten up softly in the darkness, as though one immense wave had come rippling, rippling—how far? Perhaps if you had waked up in the middle of the night you might have seen a big fish flicking in at the window and gone again. . . .

# Teaching Effective Style

Milton A. Kaplan

*The students who select the competent original from among three re-styled versions are on the way toward developing good stylistic habits of their own. This exercise comes from Mr. Kaplan of Teachers College, Columbia University, New York, New York.*

Of the four selections below, one actually appears in William Hummel and Keith Huntress, *The Analysis of Propaganda* (New York: Holt, Rinehart and Winston, Inc. 1949). The other three selections are rewritten versions, each of them revised in a different way to illustrate characteristics of poor writing. The students are asked to choose the selection that they think appears in the book.

A  There are very many avenues of communication by which propaganda reaches the unprotected ears of the innocent American public. These subtle forms of persuasion and influence are, without necessarily assigning a particular order of importance to any of them, our constant mingling with the people around us, the daily journals that inform us of domestic and world events, the periodicals that amuse and instruct us by means of stories and articles, the books that shape the pattern of our malleable minds, the broadcast programs that pour music and news into our receptive ears, and the various channels that reach our minds through the agency of our eyes; in other words, the theatre of the silver screen, the live theatre of the stage, and the television set that dispenses advertising, news, comment, and entertainment with prodigal abandon. There is nothing devastating or all-inclusive in this list of the influences on the modern mind. An examination of these influences, however, indicates that they can be separated into three distinct and distinctive categories: (1) the influences exerted by the channels of the printed words that are read, (2) the influences exerted by the channels of the spoken words that are heard, and, finally, (3) the influences exerted by the channels that transmit pictures that are seen.

B  There are a number of channels of propaganda that are important to the average American. They are, in no special order, personal contacts, newspapers, magazines, radio programs, books, and visual media, such as motion pictures, the theatre, and television. There is nothing final in the list. If you like, you may divide the propaganda that reaches you into the things you read, the things you hear, and the things you see.

C  There are an increasing number of channels of propaganda that are vitally important to the ordinary, average American. These channels, in no particular order of importance, are as follows: the numerous contacts of everyday life, the multifarious newspapers, the flourishing magazines, the radio programs that broadcast around the clock, the books that are published in ever-increasing numbers, and the visual media, such as motion pictures, the theatre, and the burgeoning television. There is nothing momentously final in this list. If you like, you may easily divide the propaganda that influences your life into the myriad things you read, the many things you hear, and the variegated things you see.

D    There are a number of channels of propaganda that are important to the average American. There are personal contacts, newspapers, magazines, radio programs, books, motion pictures, the theatre, and television. There are the things you read, the things you hear, and the things you see.

## Comment

This exercise has been used with seniors in high school, undergraduates, and graduate students. It is designed to make students aware of what good writing is. Even graduate students cling sometimes to the idea that good writing is involved and elaborate. An analysis of each selection should make the students see that good writing is simple and direct.

Selection A is very often selected by the naive and the unwary, for it sounds good. As a matter of fact, it represents an attempt to vulgarize style. A newspaper, for example, is called "the daily journal that informs us of domestic and world events." The style is swollen and pretentious, obscuring and even distorting meaning. As a result, we have a stridency of tone that is alien to the spirit of the selection.

Selection B is the original paragraph, for it is obviously the work of professional writers. The style is simple, clear, and incisive. The writers have the poise to pause occasionally for a parenthetical phrase—"if you like," for example—and to arrange their material so that the significance is revealed to the reader.

Selection C follows Selection B rather closely, but the nouns are asked to bear a heavy adjectival weight and the verbs stagger under an adverbial load. In other words, modifiers are added unnecessarily, and the result is a "padded" style.

Selection D is sometimes picked as the "best," perhaps because it is the shortest. Yet writing can be too brief and too simple. A good writer arranges details into categories that are easily discernible to the reader. In Selection D the details are simply lumped together, placing an unnecessary burden on the reader.

# Close Analysis of Style

Harold B. Stein

*Searching questions about two nonjournalistic paragraphs in a journalistic book bring out the effectiveness of certain rhetorical devices of vocabulary, sentence form, rhythm, repetition, and punctuation. There may be an indirect and salutary lesson for students—save your rule-breaking special effects until you have a worthy subject for them. Mr. Stein has retired from Williamsville Central Schools, Williamsville, New York.*

## Author's Comment
This exercise focuses attention on a number of phases of rhetoric and structure important in composition and literature. It is especially pertinent to the study of tone. To do the entire exercise will probably require several class sessions, but of course the instructor can select certain aspects for analysis, according to the needs of the class.

## Exercise
The following passages, A and B, are taken from *The Torch Is Passed* written by Saul Pett, Sid Moody, Hugh Mulligan, and Tom Henshaw and published by the Associated Press. Most of the book deals in straightforward journalistic style with the events preceding, accompanying, and following the assassination of President John F. Kennedy. Three passages (A and B below and the twenty-four paragraph concluding section) are printed in italics. Thus the typeface marks these passages off in sharp contrast to the rest of the book.

Read the two passages thoughtfully, discuss in class the questions following the passages, and see if you can decide why passages of this kind were printed differently from the rest of the book.

A     *... And the word went out from that time and place and cut the heart of a nation. In streets and offices and homes and stores, in lunch rooms and show rooms and school rooms and board*
rooms,

*on highways and prairies and beaches and mountain tops, in end-*
5  *less places crowded and sparse, near and far, white and black, Republican and Democrat, management and labor, the word went*
out

*and cut the heart of a nation. And husbands called wives and*
*wives called friends and teachers told students and motorists*
*stopped to listen on car radios and stranger told stranger.*
10 *Oh no! we cried from hearts stopped by shock, from minds fight-*
*ing the word, but the word came roaring back, true, true, true,*
*and disbelief dissolved in tears, more tears probably than this*
*nation has shed over any single event in history. Incredibly,*
*in a time of great numbers, in a time of repeated reminders that*
15 *millions would die in a nuclear war, in a time when experts*
*feared we were being numbed by numbers and immunized against*
*tragedy, the death of a single man crowded into our souls and*
*flooded our hearts and filled all the paths of our lives.*

**B**      *... A great shadow fell on the land and in the perspective of*
*death there was a great slowing down and a great stopping. The*
*farmer summoned to the house did not find the will to return to*
*the field, nor the secretary to the typewriter, nor the machin-*
5 *ist to the lathe, nor the wife to the dishes, nor the judge to*
*the bench, nor the carpenter to the saw. There was a great*
*slowing down and a great stopping and the big bronze gong*
                                                    *sounded*
*and a man shouted the market is closed and the New York Stock*
*Exchange stopped, just stopped. The Boston Symphony Orchestra*
10 *stopped a Handel concerto and started a Beethoven funeral march*
*and the Canadian House of Commons stopped and a dramatic play*
                                                          *in*
*Berlin stopped and the United Nations in New York stopped and*
*Congress and courts and schools and a race track in Rhode Island*
*and a race track in Maryland and a race track in New York stopped,*
15 *just stopped. And football games were cancelled and theaters*
*were closed and in a town called Dallas a night club called the*
*Carousel was closed by a mourner named Jack Ruby....*

## Questions on Passage A
1   Diction
   a   In the first three lines, how many words of one syllable are
       used? How many words of more than one syllable? Is this
       kind of diction effective? Why?
   b   What would be lost if the first sentence read: "... And the
       news was broadcast from that time and place and deeply
       affected a nation"?
   c   Explain the meaning and effectiveness of each of the
       following:
       1) "a time of great numbers" (line 14). (In the same sen-
          tence, what contrasts with "numbers"?)

2) "numbed by numbers" (line 16). What, besides its meaning, makes this phrase effective?

3) "immunized against tragedy" (lines 16-17). Explain the figure of speech here.

2 Rhythm

a One sentence in Lincoln's great Second Inaugural Address has been criticized because it is just like poetry and is therefore out of place and distracting in a prose passage. The sentence is: "Fondly do we hope, fervently do we pray, that this mighty scourge of war may speedily pass away." The sentence could be written as four lines of iambic-anapestic verse, as follows:

⏑ Fōnd / lў dō / wĕ hōpe
⏑ Fēr / vĕntlў dō / wĕ prāy
Thăt thĭs mĭght / ў scōurge / ŏf wār
Măy spēed / ĭlў pāss / ăwāy.

Do you agree that Lincoln's sentence is out of place in a speech? See if you can write the first sentence of Passage A as two lines of iambic-anapestic verse. Is such a sentence appropriate? Note that Lincoln's sentence has rhyme as well as meter. Does this make a difference in judging its appropriateness?

b Can you scan the first part of line 10 as a line of verse?

c What other rhythmical devices can you find in the passage? How about parallelism and repetition, for example? Find illustrations of these devices.

3 Figurative language

Explain each of the following figures of speech (a sample answer has been given for the first one; proceed in the same way with the others):

a "cut the heart of a nation" (line 1-2). ("Heart" is a common symbol for "emotions"; "cut" suggests a knife. The news of the President's death is therefore compared to a knife which cuts the heart, or in other words, causes deep sorrow.)

b "hearts stopped by shock" (line 10).

c "the word came roaring back" (line 11).

d "disbelief dissolved in tears" (line 12).

e "immunized against tragedy" (line 16-17).

  f "flooded our hearts" (line 18).
4 Other rhetorical devices
  a Comment on the use of *and* in the second sentence. Would it be better to write, in the usual manner, "streets, offices, homes, and stores"? What, exactly, would be the difference? Which would be more rhythmical? Did you include this device in your discussion of rhythm earlier in the lesson?
  b Writing involves a series of choices. The writer is committed, in the first part of a sentence or paragraph, to a specific kind of continuation. For example, if a writer begins a paragraph "There are five important values in the study of literature," we know that in the rest of the paragraph (or perhaps in the next few paragraphs) those five values will be stated. The writer has no choice: he or she is committed to this kind of continuation. Why must the writer of *A* name four types of rooms in line 3, and four types of places in line 4? When did the writer become committed to four (rather than three or five, perhaps)? Does this have to do with rhythm also?
  c In lines 5 and 6, why did the writer change from series of four members to series of two members? How are the two words in each pair related to each other? What is the author trying to make clear by using these pairs of adjectives?
  d Comment on the use of *and* in the third sentence. Usually the use of *and* in this way results in a "stringy" sentence that is childish and ineffective. Is the device effective here? If so, what makes it an exception to the usual rule?
  e Five statements are made in the third sentence. Are they arranged in any particular order? Explain.
  f What punctuation that would ordinarily be used is omitted in lines 7-9? In line 10? Do you approve of this omission? Discuss.
  g The repetition of a word or phrase at the beginning of several successive phrases or clauses is called *anaphora*. Find an example in lines 15-16. Is it effective? Why?
  h Note the repetition of "cut the heart of a nation" in the first two sentences. What has been added to the meaning of this group of words when we read it for the second time?

i   Discuss the change in point of view from third to first person. Is it effective?

## Questions on Passage B

1   Find and explain a metaphor in the first sentence. Can you find any other examples of figurative language in Passage B? How does this compare with Passage A?
2   Comment on the repetition of "great" in sentence 1.
3   What would be the difference if the first sentence read: "Many normal business, recreational, and social activities were cancelled"?
4   Explain the difference in meaning between "stopped, just stopped" in line 9 and lines 14-15 and "stopped."
5   Walt Whitman often makes use in his poetry of the "catalog," a long list of types of people and the like, as if he didn't want to leave anybody out. Is there something approaching a "catalog" in the second sentence? What *types* of occupations are actually indicated? What is the author's purpose in listing so many?
6   Compare sentence 2 with the following sentence from the Bible (Ecclesiastes 9:11):

> I returned, and saw under the sun, that the race is not to the swift, nor the battle to the strong, neither yet bread to the wise, nor yet riches to men of understanding, nor yet favor to men of skill; but time and chance happeneth to them all.

What do these sentences have in common? Do you think the writer of Passage B was deliberately imitating Biblical style?
7   The paragraph contains a number of examples of normal activities that "stopped, just stopped" after the assassination of the President. The Stock Exchange, however, is the only one that is given a sentence by itself. Why do you think the author did this?
8   Comment on the use of *and* in lines 9-17. Would it have been better, for example, to write "race tracks in Rhode Island, Maryland, and New York"? Explain your answer.
9   What punctuation, usually considered necessary, is omitted in line 8? Is the omission justified? What usual punctuation is omitted in lines 9-17? Why?
10  What would be lost if the last sentence ended: ". . . and a mourner named Jack Ruby closed a night club called the Carousel in Dallas"?

**Paragraph Structure in the Two Passages**
1    What is the topic sentence of A? How is it developed?
2    The ease of reading a paragraph seems to depend upon the repetition in most of the sentences of a key word, or at least idea. In A the key word seems to be "heart." Note how this word is repeated in four of the five sentences:
     Sentence 1—cut the *heart*
     Sentence 2—cut the *heart*
     Sentence 3—
     Sentence 4—*hearts* stopped; dissolved in *tears*
     Sentence 5—flooded our *hearts*
     The third sentence does not contain the word "heart" or a similar word. How is it related to the rest of the paragraph?
3    In Passage B, what is the topic sentence? What is the key word? Which sentences contain this key word (or a synonym)? Is there a sentence without such a word? How is it related to the rest of the paragraph?

**Comparison of the Two Paragraphs**
1    Most paragraphs are developed at least partly by examples. There are two types of examples: generalized and specific. In Passage B, "theaters were closed" is a generalized example, for no particular theater is named. But "a dramatic play in Berlin stopped" could be called a specific example, for it refers to a particular theater, even though the theater is not named.

     Which paragraph is developed entirely by generalized examples? Which paragraph contains both generalized and specific examples? Can you explain this difference in style?

2    What other differences in style can you find? Which paragraph makes effective use of contrast? Which paragraph consists entirely of loose sentences? Which combines loose and periodic sentences? Which passage makes a greater use of figurative language? Which, on the whole, employs simpler diction? Which makes more use of repetition?
3    What is the tone of each paragraph? What is the purpose of each—to give information, or convey a mood, or something else? Can you now answer our original question as to why these passages were printed differently from the rest of the book?

4 We have seen that both passages violate several of the "rules" of writing that appear in college and high school textbooks. Below are some of the violations of rule in these passages:

Omission of needed commas and quotation marks
Connecting too many clauses with *and*
Too much repetition
Wordiness ("a town called Dallas" etc.)

Yet these passages represent good writing. Does this mean that the "rules" are wrong? Do you think any rule of writing is valid 100 percent of the time? Do you think many rules are valid most of the time? Do some of the rules depend upon the purpose of the writing and the style being used?

Note: In Lloyd Lewis's fascinating book *Myths After Lincoln* you will find complete story of the assassination of Lincoln and its effect on the nation. Lincoln's funeral train toured the cities of the North for more than two weeks, being greeted by thousands of weeping people in each city. More than seven million people saw Lincoln's coffin. Lewis compares the Lincoln myth to the myth of the dying god as explained in Sir James Frazer's famous book *The Golden Bough.* Lincoln was killed on Good Friday, and many clergymen in the North compared his death to that of Christ. In many ways, Lewis's book provides an interesting comparison with accounts of the assassination of President Kennedy.

# Imitating Styles

Littleton Long

*Although keyed here to world masterworks, the selection of characteristic devices of subject and style and the imitation of these devices in subject matter of the students' own choosing can apply to any literature of any period. Mr. Long teaches at the University of Vermont, Burlington, Vermont.*

If in later years college graduates are described as "solid and dependable, but lacking in vision," it may be partly because the first two qualities were called upon over and over in essays, term papers, lab reports, and examinations, while the third was neglected. Only those relatively few students who take creative courses in writing or the arts get much opportunity to exercise their imaginations. Therefore, to foster use of the imagination under controlled circumstances, I make sure that my students write one paper each semester specifically designed as work in applied imagination, rather than the usual critical essays. The topics mentioned below require the student to select those elements of style and those attitudes of mind that characterize the author, work, and culture. Then the student must imitate that style and attitude while writing on some topic he or she knows well. These imitations are not parodies, for they do not mock the original author; nor are they old-fashioned exercises in rhetoric, for elements of style to be imitated are not pointed out while the class works on the author in question. Here are half a dozen topics I have tried out over the years.

1  After the class had studied Virgil's *Aeneid*, I asked for a description of a nontheological Elysian Fields that would reflect American cultural goals and favorite activities as Virgil's Book VI reflects Roman goals, interests, and standards. Freed from theological considerations, many students wrote satirically tinged sketches of an all-too-comfortable, conformist, materialistic society busy in collecting and showing off its possessions.

2  After students had spent a week on Juvenal's *Satires* (including No. 6 "Against Women"), I asked for a Juvenalian satire on college students of the opposite sex. In doing this assignment the students should show that Juvenal, though he exaggerates and raises preposterous rhetorical questions, voices his very personal views (plenty of *I*'s, plenty of ire) and paints the scene with every line.

3  Dante's *Inferno* can evoke an Academic Inferno, divided like his, into three major categories with subdivisions ad lib. Here the paper's goal should be to imitate Dante's logic rather than his style. Students should be warned not to "please the teacher"; otherwise papers come in indicating that cutting classes is the most heinous academic crime. One should also outlaw misdemeanors (speeding, etc.) that have no connection with academic life; plenty of peccadilloes remain. I ask

for an outline or sketch of the whole Academic Inferno in brief form, but require the student to write out in detail a description of crimes and their appropriate punishments for *one* of the three infernal areas. This topic, sometimes ingeniously keyed to the locale or to specific campus buildings, elicits fiendish glee.

4  An assignment to write "One More Adventure of Don Quixote" has produced some papers of limited value. Students, for example, wrote of beating, bashing, cracked crowns, and missing molars. Alert students, however, may exhibit with some sensitivity or good humor the illusion-reality theme, or make the reader sigh and smile because society is unperfected still.

5  Essays imitating Voltaire's *Candide* have been quite successful. With their imitative effort keyed to the local winter carnival, students describing "How Candide Took Cunegonde to the Best of All Possible Kakewalks" let their imaginations run riot in exaggerated wry disasters, swift pace of incident, topical satire, and rational attacks on irrational behavior or thinking that they have encountered.

6  The non-narrative style of Melville, rising from firm facts to airy nebulosities and by turns allusive, rhythmic, grandiose, realistic, oratorical, proves a real challenge to students. I urge them to select topics on which Melville would have lavished exuberantly his sardonic wit and anti-materialistic spleen.

# Ideas for Whole Papers and Special Topics

This section presents some good excuses for writing—exercises that blend freedom and control, imagination and format, and face the writer with rather specific challenges whose keynote is variety. Then follow exercises in the standard and essential categories of Description, Research, and the Short Story. Student and teacher alike may well find these among the most challenging and original exercises in the whole collection.

# Depicting American Character

Raymond S. Goodlatte

*This assignment seems aimed at separating the facile generalization from the sound, well-grounded one. It asks the student to take particular pains to unify the essay metaphorically and in tone. Mr. Goodlatte submitted this exercise from the Putney School, Putney, Vermont.*

**Author's Comment**

All good writing is the making of definition; whether poem or essay it is an "effort to express a knowledge imperfectly felt, to articulate relationships not quite seen, to make or discover some pattern in the world." In short, what is creative in writing is the completion it brings to some manner of experience. I have used this assignment several times both at Harvard and at Putney without observing any diminution of freshness—or even becoming bored with the papers. One object is to suggest that, in a sense, any society is provincial.

The initial writing exercise, with which we are concerned during the first two weeks of school while the students are making their own preliminary readings of the novel assigned for intensive study, is an essay (500-1000 words) on some aspect of the American character. Together in class we read E. M. Forster's superb "Notes on the English Character" (*Abinger Harvest*, Harcourt, 1936, pp. 3-15). Forster's essay serves us all as a point of reference, suggests in what sense a people may be said to possess a national character, and provides an example of suitable analysis and criticism. The assignment affords excellent opportunity to discuss the ambiguous matter of the validity of generalizations, the "tone of voice" in which Forster makes his few very broad generalizations, the proper use of extended metaphor, and other genuine problems of the artist and thinker.

Forster has the space to develop a number of aspects of the English character, relating them all to what he diagnoses as an "undeveloped heart." I ask my students to write on *one* aspect of the American character only, and to indicate, preferably without making an explicit statement, whether they consider it a salient

74

aspect of the national character or, perhaps, merely an amusing, if widely shared, foible.

Some objections I try to anticipate. America may be made up of many diverse peoples, but immigration has been rigidly restricted for some time now, and even a melting pot melts down to *something.* A lively class discussion of in what senses America may be called a young country and in what senses a mature one, serves to scotch a great many invalid assertions and much repetitious reading. Students who feel that they should know other countries in order to talk about this one are reminded that a true insight into the American character is not the less true if applicable to all humanity, that analysis and description need not be comparative.

Along with a selection of the students' papers I read a few of Alistair Cooke's broadcast essays (*One Man's America*). I ask students to write from their own observations, but the exercise stimulates a good deal of "outside reading" *after* the completion of the papers. Among the books I have suggested are *Babbitt; U.S.A.; Winesburg, Ohio; Middletown* and *Middletown in Transition;* the Beards' *Rise of American Civilization;* Peter H. Odegard's *The American Public Mind;* Frederick Turner's *Frontier in American History;* Parrington's *Main Currents in American Thought;* various novels of Henry James; works in American philosophy (I save Santayana's "The Genteel Tradition in American Philosophy" for use at another time); and works by a number of hands on other national characters.

# New Dimensions in Understanding

Alice Baldwin

*Less rigorously tied to writing than most, this exercise stimulates real imaginative endeavor to get at the heart of a concept through five different media. Ms. Baldwin formerly taught at the Northfield School for Girls, Northfield, Massachusetts.*

What color is "Love"? What shape is "Greed"? What sound has "Pride"?

Quite sensible questions. Far more sensible, actually, than the ones students ask when they study poetry:

"Do poets think about these principles when they write?"

"Do painters remember all that stuff about balance and contrast and so on when they're painting?"

"Gosh, writing a symphony must be like doing math."

Then there is the lank, blank look when first the class encounters:

> If they be two, they are two so
> As stiff twin compasses are two,
> Thy soul the fixed foot, makes no show
> To move, but doth, if th'other do.

"What's it mean?????"

Scholars say that present-day artists have lost touch with the masses, and vice versa. In sophomore English at Northfield and junior English at Mount Hermon, we have conducted a project that will, we hope, shove the students a few steps down the road to understanding. Here's how our project works.

We give a list of words: names of the emotions, or names of the seven sins and the seven virtues. Each member of the class selects a word and keeps it secret. They must tell no one which word they have selected. They are then given a code number to use in place of their own name. Their work will be signed with the code number so that they need not feel self-conscious.

They try, next, to express their word—without ever mentioning the word itself—in five media: clay, flat composition (paint or pastel), musical theme or melodic line, narrative incident, and lyric poem.

Their problem is twofold. They have to find a fresh, original, individual approach. At the same time they must try to communicate their idea to other members of the class.

Their reaction is likely to be either/or. Either they look horror-stricken, or they look pleased, thinking, "This'll be a snap." We say nothing—simply make the assignment as an outside project and go about our routine classroom business: grammar, composition, introduction to poetry. We do pause, however, to point out that we are attacking the problem backwards: that we are asking them to create from a general meaning a particular interpretation, whereas the great artist often starts with the particular and moves toward the general.

Aha! In no time at all, the students have discovered why they need the basic principles of art. They bring in their first efforts: stiff, conventional, careful. And dull.

Then we must use three or four class periods to do some spadework. First, we take the students to the art lab where our art instructor, Mr. Jones, acquaints them with the various media in his department; illustrates the methods involved in their use; and applies the principles of art to pictures, a representational painting and an abstract, perhaps. He spreads a table before them with the tools of his trade and says that they may use whatever they want, whenever they want.

Immediately they are firing questions at him and tinkering with the clay or the brushes. They know from his easy manner that he will help them without crushing their spirits under discouraging criticism. And—where an hour before they stood on a darkling plain—they now begin to see light.

Another period must be spent on music. We take the same principles of art that Mr. Jones lined out for us and apply them to musical composition. We differentiate between "theme" and "melody." We give a brief and elementary lecture, illustrated on the nearest piano, of tonality and the use of scales and chord progressions in Occidental musical composition. We note the effects obtained in different pitch, tone, and tempo. Then, perhaps, we play Prokofieff's "Peter and the Wolf," or Brahms' Fourth, or Beethoven's Fifth, or Stravinsky's "Firebird Suite."

Thus, in a few periods, we have made a hasty dash through three of the five assigned fields of endeavor, giving (we hope) enough information to challenge, not enough to inhibit. As for the writing assignment—the narrative and lyric—we can work into our daily English class time the principles and techniques involved in writing. We make reference when possible to their unit. We might even take several daring first efforts, discuss them in class, criticize, analyze, subject them to the scrutiny of the entire class, and return them for revision.

First efforts are likely to be hollow imitations of Eugene Field or the latest sermon. Once this is pointed out to young artists, they gather up their work, hurt and huffy. But! They start at once on new drafts, new experiments. They are learning to criticize their work. Their own words are no longer "deathless prose." And furthermore, they learn that it's an enjoyable experience—to be able to criticize oneself. Once we see students analyze their own work, we can relax. Hereafter our job is not to criticize, but only to question. If we get a good sound answer, we're satisfied. After all, we're not trying to make an artistic genius out of every member of the class.

Now we begin to get more originality, more freedom. Here comes "Anger" as a big red splotch that sprays out over the black background of an oil. Here we get "Faith" as a blue mountain, crossed intermittently with clouds in hot colors, but reaching upward through them. Here we get "Grief" in clay: a gladiator bowed in an arch, with a hole cut through his back. Here someone writes for "Hope," "The sun cannot be stained . . ." and for "Avarice," "fingers crab-like scrape the money in. . . ." Here someone weighs and balances "Justice" with gong-like chords that rise and fall. Someone else tape-records seven whole minutes of original music. Here a student, dissatisfied with the imitative quality of a first painting, brings in four more that were done "just for fun"; all four show a boldness of conception, a release of creativity which certainly pays part of a teacher's salary.

Paintings are repainted, clay is remodeled, music is retranscribed, compositions are re- and rewritten. By choice. Not by force.

The school library exhibits the projects. Then the students see what they do in surroundings different from the classroom, get a new perspective, and often drag away something to improve it yet again. They cringe at some questions they hear asked. They are delighted and thrilled with comments that come from elders, from guests or alumnae, perhaps. They may also have a sneaking suspicion that the way the library has handled their works makes them look a lot better than they really are. But isn't that nice?

Once the five media have been explored, they have one more paper to do. They write an essay in which they explain their choice of subject matter, describe what they did in each medium and why, analyze the results, decide how they were limited by the medium and what possibilities they found in it, sum up their efforts, and state what they have learned.

Finally all the work is gathered up. The girls send theirs to the boys' classes, and the boys send theirs to the girls' classes. More discussion and analysis follow, uninhibited, and spiced with a bit of mystery, since identities are still hidden under code numbers. Some surprising things are revealed. Girls are far more logical, reasonable, and analytical than boys ever before realized. Boys are far more original and imaginative than girls ever before realized. We have heard boys say, "These girls are really whips!" We have heard girls say, "How can boys do such a wonderful job of writing about women?" All have a new respect for one another and considerable mutual admiration.

How is all this subjective work marked? Since we are English teachers, we have no trouble marking the three literary efforts. Since we are not artists or musicians, we do not mark efforts in these fields until we have read the final essay. Then we must look again at the clay, paint, and music and decide whether the student has achieved what he or she set out to do and whether that student has been honest in his or her interpretations.

What have they learned? Specifically, they have learned quite a lot about certain aspects of vocabulary: basic meanings, connotations, contexts, emphasis. Second, they have learned what imagery is, both visual and auditory. Third, they have learned symbolism, both conventional and nonconventional. Fourth, they know rhythm, balance, contrast, proportion, transition, unity, coherence. Fifth, they have made halting steps toward understanding a higher level of art, music, and literature.

In addition, there are dozens of little odds and ends they have picked up here and there. They saw early in the game, for instance, how a virtue could be twisted into sin, but a sin could never honestly be turned into virtue. They saw how virtues and sins and emotions overlap, that in the presentation of one there may be overtones or suggestions of another. They learned that a painting can be "read" just as a poem can be read. They learned that the artist in any field presupposes a willingness on the part of the audience to help re-enact the creative process, and that the audience must exercise the intellect in order to do so.

And what about the teachers? We have had an exercise in self-control, certainly. We have had to refrain from conventional criticism, limit ourselves to questions. "Why did you use curved lines here?" "Why did you choose three-quarter time?" "Why has this image suggested itself to you?" We cannot assist. Not really. The students must plumb their own depths, their own experience. Not ours. But when the frowning frustration on one young face suddenly changes to a grin and a glow, we know we've done a little work in a sixth medium; for teaching is creative art, too. In what other unit of work, for instance, has a student willingly written the same theme four times over? In what other unit has he or she been so intent upon defending a choice with logical explanation and clear, cold reason?

From the purely personal viewpoint, we've learned a lot, too. We may have dipped our hands into the clay pot, or swiped our sleeves across our own palettes; and quite possibly we've had a whack at transcribing music. We've been stimulated to research and study and thought. After all, if someone asks, "What color is 'Fortitude'?" or, "What shape is 'Sorrow'?" how can we answer?

# The Chinese Eight-Legged Essay

Richard P. Benton

*Though the historical background may not be available in every library, the essence of this exercise comes through clearly enough. Surely it will be the most unusual assignment the class is likely to have all year. Its demands as controlled writing will test your best and titilate the most blasé writer in class. Mr. Benton teaches at Trinity College, Hartford, Connecticut.*

Under the Chinese Empire the Eight-Legged Essay (*pa-ku wên-chang*) was the principal road both to literary honors and to an official career by virtue of the civil service examination system then in effect. Devised in 1487, when specific requirements for the form of essays in the Chinese civil service examinations were laid down by the authorities, the Eight-Legged Essay was so called because there were eight specific steps or "legs" in the development of its composition.

There were also other specifications. The topic to be developed was a quotation taken from the Confucian classics. The length was also usually specified and varied from about 350 to 700 words. Certain stylistic features were also demanded, such as parallelism and harmonious contrast.

From the early years of the Ming Dynasty (1368-1643), candidates in the examinations were required to write three essays on the Four Books of Confucius and four essays on the Five Classics. However, the writing of the Eight-Legged Essay was not the only requirement in passing the literary examinations, for the candidates were also obliged to compose two kinds of poems: the *lu shih,* or five- or seven-word regulated poem, and the *fu,* or irregular but metrical and rhyming composition.

According to Professor Ch'en Shou-Yi, the literary historian, the Chinese Eight-Legged Essay was a very important literary genre during the Chinese Empire "which engaged the universal attention of the literati for five centuries and which dominated the main stream of literary production."

I decided that I might stimulate my students and refresh their interest in essay writing by giving them an exercise in the writing of the Chinese Eight-Legged Essay. The results I obtained justified my decision. My students not only became highly interested in trying to conform to the requirements and objective of the Eight-Legged Essay, but also developed an additional interest in Chinese education and in the civil service examination system that used to prevail in China. This additional interest furnished worthwhile topics for the regular essays that followed the exercise in the Eight-Legged Essay.

1 Describe to the students the civil service examination system in effect during the Chinese Empire and the importance of the Eight-Legged Essay in that system. Adequate preparation for this step can be done by reading pp. 546-560 of Vol. I of S. W. Williams' *The Middle Kingdom* (New York, 1883); the chapter "Civil Service Examinations," pp. 308-328 of W. A. P. Martin's *The Lore of Cathay or the Intellect of China* (Edinburgh and London, 1901); and the chapter "The Examination Life of the Gentry in Nineteenth-Century China," pp. 165-209 of Chung-li Chang's *The Chinese Gentry, Studies on Their Role in Nine-teenth-Century Chinese Society* (Seattle, Wash., 1955). A discussion of the important influence that China's examination system had on the West can be found in Ssu-yü Têng's essay, "China's Examination System and the West," which is included in *China,* edited by Harley Farnsworth MacNair (Berkeley and Los Angeles, 1946), pp. 441-451.

2 Duplicate the following English translation of a typical Eight-Legged Essay which was originally written by the Chinese scholar Wang Ao, who flourished during the late fifteenth and early sixteenth centuries, and present copies to the students. The eight "legs" or principal divisions of the essay are indicated by Arabic figures in parentheses. The topic of the essay is a quotation from the Confucian *Analects* (Lun Yü), XII, ix. Naturally, the stylistic features of parallelism and harmonious contrast in the original Chinese are not altogether apparent in the translation. The translation is as follows:

(Topic) "If the people have plenty, how can the ruler not have plenty?"

1) When the people below are prosperous, the ruler above will necessarily be prosperous.

2) Since the ruler's wealth is stored up by the people, how is it reasonable that the ruler alone should be poor?

3) In his message to Duke Ai, Yu Jo spoke profoundly when he broached the idea that the ruler and the ruled are one body. He suggested that the Duke had increased taxes because state revenues had been insufficient. Although as a practical matter the Duke wanted his state expenditures to be sufficient, what could take precedence over his providing for the sufficiency of his people?

4) If the farm lands were tithed with the object of continually maintaining economy in expenditure and bestowing love on the people, taking one tenth of their unused agriculture produce, then the people's exertions would benefit them instead of being eaten up in taxes. The people would have what they earn, and their wealth would not be exhausted. They would store up grain in their households. They would be able to serve their parents and to support their wives and children without being distressed. They would be able to keep their houses in repair and their streams bridged. They would be able to take care of the living and to bury the dead without being anxious.

5) If the people have plenty, how should the ruler alone be poor?

6) The ruler always has access to what is stored in the households without its being hoarded in the treasury so that he can say, "This is my wealth." What is distributed among the farm houses and the fields the ruler can always obtain without its being piled up in the public granary so that he can claim, "These hoardings are mine." With inexhaustible availability, what need is there to worry if the demands are not immediately met; with inexhaustible resources, why be troubled if projects remain incomplete?

7) Sacrificial animals and ritual grain are abundant and quite sufficient for worship. There are baskets full of jade and silks which are quite sufficient for paying tribute and giving presents at court to maintain honor. If they are not sufficient every day, the people themselves will provide them. In what will there be a shortage? There are breakfasts and suppers, beefs and sweet wines which are quite sufficient to meet the needs

of visitors. There are carriages and military arms and equipment which are quite sufficient to prepare and to put military expeditions into the field. If these things are not available every day, the people themselves will naturally supply them. Again, in what will there be insufficiency?

8) Alas! The original motive in establishing the tithing system was so that the people and the nation would be prosperous. How does it follow that taxes ought to be increased to secure national income?

3 Describe to the students the eight-part structure of the essay by Wang Ao, giving the terminology for each "leg" or division and explaining the part each plays in the development of the topic. In Chinese the topic is called the *chu t'i*. The first "leg" is called the *p'o t'i*, which means "the breaking open of the topic." The second "leg" is called the *ch'êng t'i*, which means "accepting the topic." The third division is called the *ch'i chiang*, which means "embarking on the topic." The fourth division is called the *ch'i ku*, which means "introductory corollary." The fifth division is called the *hsü ku*, which means "first middle leg." The sixth division is called the *chung ku*, which means "second middle leg." The seventh division is called the *hou ku*, which means "first final leg." And the eighth division is called the *chieh shu*, which means "tying the knot." For a further discussion of the structure of the Chinese Eight-Legged Essay see Ch'ên Shou-Yi, *Chinese Literature, A Historical Introduction* (New York, 1961), pp. 505-510. Professor Ch'ên has also translated Wang Ao's essay. For translations of other such essays see F. S. A. Bourne, " 'Essay of a Provincial Graduate,' with Translation," *The China Review,* VIII, No. 6 (May/June, 1880), pp. 352-355; and S. W. Williams, *The Middle Kingdom* (New York, 1883), Vol. I, pp. 554-556.

4 Give the students a one-sentence quotation and have them write an essay in imitation of the Chinese Eight-Legged Essay, using the quoted sentence as a topic. A length of 500 words is recommended.

**Additional Comment**

I wish to acknowledge here my indebtedness to Professor Ch'ên of Pomona College who so kindly gave me a copy of Wang Ao's essay in the original Chinese and informed me of several technical terms which I did not know. His translation of Wang Ao's essay was also very helpful to me in making my own translation.

As I suggested at the beginning, after the students have done their exercise in the Chinese Eight-Legged Essay, topics for regular essays in the course can be gleaned by having them read the source materials which I have listed.

# Writing as Problem Solving

Donald C. Stewart

*Three innovative writing exercises ask the student to look at life in America as people relax, experience the heterogeneity of living, and link (or fail to link) ethics with living. Originally at the University of Illinois, Mr. Stewart now teaches at Kansas State University, Manhattan, Kansas.*

**Author's Comment**
The following exercises, though traditional in form, have generated intelligent and imaginative student writing for two reasons: (1) they have confronted students with intriguing variations on old patterns, and (2) they have taught them the thought processes involved in solving the problems posed by these patterns.

**Exercise 1  An Assignment in Description**
Imagine that you are a twentieth-century Gulliver. You have been shipwrecked and now find yourself forced by circumstances to live in a strange land called Illinois. Specifically, you are living in an urban center named Champaign-Urbana. While you are in this strange city, you take time to observe the customs of a unique group of persons in the society, a group identified as "college students." In the hope that someday you will return to your native land and report your observations of these college students to your countrymen, you prepare written accounts of the activities of this group. One of your most interesting papers describes a custom associated with an event the students call "Homecoming." Unfortunately, none of the students will interpret the custom for you. All your report contains is a description of the

custom together with your interpretation of what it means. (You may assume that you have sufficient facility in the language to communicate with natives. But remember, none will *interpret* any aspect of Homecoming for you.)

Your assignment is to prepare that report. However, let me emphasize one point. If you merely describe Homecoming, or any part of it, without careful consideration of the way in which you are to do it, you will not have fulfilled the assignment. You must play the role I have prescribed. To get yourself in the frame of mind necessary to do this, I suggest that you read some pages of *Gulliver's Travels* or Butler's *Erewhon.*

### Comment
The point here is to test not only the range and quality of the students' perceptions and their ability to organize them (the usual goal of an assignment in description), but, more important, their objectivity about the culture in which they live. The better the student, the more successfully he or she will make the imaginative leap required to take the point of view required here. The assignment also tests students' classifying ability. They cannot use the term "football game," for example. They must decide what class of things it belongs to and identify it as such.

### Exercise 2   An Assignment in Classification

shaving mug
typewriter
three wine bottles
a ream of yellow paper
a set of screwdrivers
one orange tree
a clarinet
three pieces of lumber,
    walnut, 1" x 6"
a tube of toothpaste
a cigarette holder

a flannel shirt
a notebook
a twelve-volume history
    of the United States
bubble bath
vitamin pills
plant food
a package of sugarless
    chewing gum
a toupee

Listed above are approximately twenty unrelated items. You are to create a narrative incident in which you can mention *all* the items under certain categories, which you will invent to serve your purpose. Limit the narrative, however. Use it only as a tool for setting up the categories under which you can assemble these disparate items.

## Comment
Traditionally, exercises of this type ask students to classify people, buildings, cars, etc., things for which categories already exist. My assignment gives them a horrendous collection of articles and asks them to invent categories. As they do this, they begin to see how arbitrarily, at times, people impose order on the world.

### Exercise 3    An Argument
Mr. Music, a dealer in stringed instruments (violins, violas, violoncellos, etc.) learns from a friend that Mr. Gullible, owner of a Kentucky estate, wishes to sell a number of violins and bows. When Mr. Music arrives at Mr. Gullible's estate, he discovers that Gullible wants approximately $200 more than the ten violins he is selling are worth. However, he is willing to throw in the bows as part of the deal. Mr. Music immediately accepts. What Gullible does not know is that six of the ten bows are extremely fine sticks, that each will bring at least $1000. The ethical problem is this: Should Mr. Music tell Mr. Gullible the value of his bows, or should he buy them without telling him, as he does? Your essay is to be a defense of or an attack on Mr. Music's actions. Your paper will be graded on the perception you show in exploring the many aspects of this problem and on the rhetorical skill which you demonstrate in presenting your argument.

## Comment
Exercises in argument for freshman students should never proceed from generalities. Titles like "Why I Oppose Our Country's Stand in Viet Nam" inevitably produce the unsupported generalities with which composition teachers are all too familiar. This exercise involves the students in an immediate problem, a specific act, which they are to judge. To it they will bring their whole system of values and their knowledge of economic theory in the Western world. Most important, it denies them the opportunity to equivocate. They must commit themselves to a position, then construct a defense of that position. An additional benefit of this assignment is the problem it poses in assessing evidence. For example, is Gullible's $200 overcharge an attempt to cheat the dealer or is it ignorance? Before committing themselves, good students ponder carefully the many implications of such facts.

# Write Your Own Obituary

Richard D. Kepes

*Another unusual writing assignment should stimulate students'*
*imaginations and let them write, in a controlled style, on one of their*
*favorite subjects, themselves. Mr. Kepes teaches at St. Lawrence Uni-*
*versity, Canton, New York.*

**Exercise**

Write your own obituary as it might appear in the *New York Times*
at some future date of your own choosing.

**Comment**

I discovered this composition idea while practicing various types
of current writing with a college composition course. Bright college seniors had no trouble duplicating the obituary writing con-
ventions of the *New York Times.* However, when asked to write a
longer obituary—their own—they wrote enthusiastically. Their
lives, it turned out, were uniformly successful, with brilliant
careers for themselves and their mates.

Since I believe that all young people spend much time musing
about their futures, this ostensibly fanciful exercise lets students
express some of their most closely held imaginings without embarrassment. I believe that the student who would botch "My
Dream of Tomorrow" or "My Purpose in Life" is much more comfortable protected by the format which begins—"John Doe, a
popular singer of the 1970s, died yesterday at his home. . . ."

More recently, I used the assignment with high school age students at the Phillips Exeter Academy Summer School. Although
the students were allowed a large part of a class period in which
to write, one boy, who had made assorted noises indicating pleasure while he wrote, continued well beyond the end of the class
period. I expected to read some fantastic detailing of space voy-
ages or film stardom, but he had written a straightforward account of his education in college and medical school, his gradual
takeover of his father's medical practice, professional and char-
itable organizations which he had joined or headed, and honors
which had come to him. As he left he said, "Best assignment of
the summer."

This assignment does seem pleasurable to students, a worthwhile end in itself. It can also be used for practice in noneditorial journalistic style. I've learned a great deal about my students from it, too.


# Be It Ever So Humble,
# They *Can*
# Go Home Again

Lynn Z. Bloom

*Wide possibilities inhere in this assignment where observation, comparison, generalization, and interpretation make heavy (and agreeable) demands on the writer. Ms. Bloom now teaches at the University of New Mexico, Albuquerque, New Mexico.*

I like to help beginning composition students feel comfortable by allowing them to write on a subject they know well. But because I also want their intellectual and literary skills to grow, I cannot allow them to rewarm old chestnuts, no matter how cosy they feel by the familiar fireside. For the past several years I have given an ostensibly simple writing assignment within the first month of the first semester of Freshman English that employs more skills of writing and logical analysis than the students may realize, that almost all of them enjoy writing—perhaps because it's so close to home?—and that is fascinating to read, in the variety of judgments and personalities expressed therein.

I ask the students to communicate the *human* essence of the dwellings they live in, by transforming their residences from the realtor's "3 br. sp lev, lr fp, a/c, mort assum" into real homes with real people in them.

The first part of the paper is to "Describe in detail your home dwelling and contrast it with a quite different house well known to you, inhabited by persons other than you or your family, unless you obtain the instructor's permission to discuss two different dwellings of your family at different stages in their lives. Include primarily those physical details which you see as clues to the occupants' values, personalities, interests, interpersonal relationships, life style(s)." The second part requests, "On the basis of these details, compare and contrast the inhabitants of the respective homes, commenting on their values, personalities, interpersonal relationships, individual and collective (family or other group) goals, life styles. If you don't want to write on your house, compare, contrast and analyze (in the same fashion specified for the houses) two other buildings well known to you, such as two churches or school buildings." Other structures may be substituted, for it's not fair to put students, who might be ashamed about or humiliated by discussing a deteriorating dwelling or family situation, or even those who might be suffering from an embarrassment of riches, on the spot by forcing them to write about their own homes if they'd rather not. The main criterion for selection is that the physical details of the buildings must reflect the users' tastes, values, and so on.

This assignment provides the students with practice in various aspects of composition. Obviously, it requires description—careful attention to detail. ("Our furniture is Early American" or "Mediterranean," or "Middle Salvation Army"—but precisely *what* furniture, and how does it look?) Meaningful description also involves a sense of the gestalt, of the forest and the trees, and the ability to discriminate between what is significant and what is not. For instance, the writers need not indicate the dimensions of each room (though they should specify what they mean by such relative terms as "large," "expensive," "modern," etc.), but they do need to make the readers visualize the residence according to its dominant and significant aspects. This will probably require a detailed description of some or all of the following features: cost; style of architecture or furniture; presence or absence of areas for work, recreation; focal point of the house (kitchen, family room, garden); state of repair; neatness or messiness; color scheme; prominence and significance of artifacts (paintings, books, trophies, mementoes). The milieu—urban, suburban, rural—environs, and grounds should be noted, as well as whether the dwelling is a house, apartment, condominium, trailer, or other sort.

Both parts of the assignment also involve comparison and contrast between both dwellings and their respective inhabitants. This may require classification as well: "My family has many material possessions; John's has very few, except for several hundred books."

So much for the obvious. More subtly, the assignment has other attributes that enhance the students' analytic and stylistic abilities, but which might alarm them if they heard them called by their technical labels. This is an exercise in inductive reasoning, for it requires the evidence to be included and analyzed, and conclusions to be drawn from it: "The presence in the garage of two air-conditioned Buicks, five bicycles, a Honda, and a Sailfish reveal my family to be economically well-to-do, fond of outdoor exercise, and enjoying physical comfort." How technical our discussion of the process of inductive reasoning becomes is determined each year by the level of sophistication of the class; sometimes I wait until I return the papers to tell them what they've done.

Students need to be reminded that they must present evidence to demonstrate their conclusions, and that these conclusions should be the only or most likely ones that can be derived from the evidence. Thus if the student's clothes closet contains only a few, utilitarian outfits, does it mean that he or she is poor? a hippie? unostentatious? rebelling against parents he or she considers overly materialistic? practicing a religious faith that calls for simplicity or uniformity of garments? indifferent to conventions of style? living in a hot climate where people wear very little? They will need to supply other sorts of corroborating information before an unequivocal conclusion can be drawn. We spend considerable discussion (say, a class hour) on this and on other aspects of the paper while the students are working on it, to make sure they understand what they're doing.

This paper, like all writings, requires an adjustment of tone to content. The first part is likely to be more objective than the second, though both parts could be successfully connotative if the writer were unusually skilled. He or she may have to be cautioned against sentimentality, which might work at cross-purposes to important points if it moved the readers to ridicule, for this paper, like others, requires the author to be continually aware of the audience. Perhaps no one in the class has ever seen the writer's house or met the family. Therefore the writer, and the writer alone, must perform the introductions graphically and precisely.

This the students usually do, and so the assignment has been very successful. The students also enjoy writing and discussing it; after all, they're experts on their own castles. I often ask them to make two carbons and exchange and examine these papers in groups of three or four. Having an identifiable and immediate audience in addition to the instructor helps the students to be more responsible as writers and as readers, in addition to introducing them to each other. The paper and ensuing discussion also cause them to take a fresh and more objective look at the nest from which they've just flown (or in which they're still ensconced), and a closer view of how others live. So in these respects the assignment promotes the students' personal growth and maturity, as well as their literary development.

Each year, after reading this set of graphic and often witty papers, I feel that I know the students so well that I am tempted to invite them over for a reciprocal look at my house, with its book-lined family room, its comfortable cherry wood kitchen, and its study strewn with casually-piled projects. And sometimes I do just that.

# Getting Students to
# Use Detail

Fredrica K. Bartz

*Narrative springing out of observation is subjected to interrogation until writers get used to supplying sufficient concreteness and specificity. Ms. Bartz contributed this assignment from the University of Michigan at Flint, Michigan.*

If you have despaired of ever getting your students to embellish the monotonous gray tones of their prose with specific and colorful detail, you might try a device that has worked very well with students in our remedial writing laboratory. It is a game that not only teaches the art of being specific and graphic, but also leaves students looking forward to the next writing session.

You begin the exercise by giving the students a cartoon or a picture depicting a situation about which it is easy to conjecture a background. One of my favorites is a cartoon showing two castles with a valley in between. On the balcony of one a king, queen, and various personages are standing by the prince and his bride, the neighboring princess. The prince is saying, "There's really not much to tell. I just grew up and married the girl next door."

We talk a little about what it would be like to grow up a prince and about how a prince might go about courting a princess. After a little discussion, the class is asked to write a narrative detailing something about the boy's and girl's backgrounds, about their meeting, and about the courting (where they went, what they did, etc.).

The next day I divide the class into groups of from three to five people. I ask how long it would normally take to read one person's narrative to the group. Most guess about two or three minutes. Then I tell them that *today* will be different because the rest of the group will be interrupting constantly to ask questions, every question they can think of. What color was the girl's hair? Were the boy's black shoes shiny or dull? Why did the girl's uncle want to buy them a Volkswagen rather than a Buick? How far was it to the drive-in? In other words, the group wants to know everything about everything.

The object of the game is to think of so many questions that the person who is reading cannot finish his or her narrative within a set time limit, say, fifteen minutes. Each time a question is asked, the person must stop and fill in that detail (actually writing it in on the paper). If the group can prevent the reader from getting to the end of the paper by asking enough questions, they each get two points. If the person can get to the end, he or she gets six points. The game generally gets exciting.

Playing this composition game accomplishes two things; first, it shows students how much detail they can actually produce, and second, it motivates them to try for it. The second time the game is played, you will see your students working hard at getting in as much specific and graphic detail as they can think of, trying to anticipate and frustrate the inexorable interrogators. Subsequent games should be used to help students understand the function of detail in controlling a story's progress, tone, structure, etc. Part of the game rules might include a point system which awards points to the storyteller if he or she is merely being asked for padding by the interrogators. As the students continue to write, they will hopefully not lose the outpouring of details which the game initially encourages, but will be better able to select the details which clearly and effectively tell their particular story. It is important for the teacher to emphasize that it is the quality of the details that matters, not the quantity; and to shift the emphasis ultimately from winning the game to an involvement with good writing. As both parts of the process can be satisfying, this type of exercise should prove enjoyable for student and teacher alike.

# Writing from Literature

Valerie Goldzung

*Furnishing a personality around whom to build narrative, description, drama, exposition, or argument facilitates student writing by setting up boundaries within which the imaginative and creative abilities can flourish. Ms. Goldzung sent this from Springfield College, Springfield, Massachusetts.*

One of the problems with using a reader in a composition course is the temptation for both teachers and students to talk about the themes and ideas in a work they are reading rather than to use it as an aid in discussing rhetoric, or, in an introductory course in literature, as a way to concentrate on forms. After all, it's much more fun to talk about "life" than literary and rhetorical abstractions, even if you're using examples. One of the ways I've tried to enliven discussions of rhetorical and literary problems of form and style is by using the things we are reading simply as common material for imaginative productions of the students themselves—short stories, skits, interviews.

I had always been struck by the ability of students, myself included, to write with color and concreteness when consciously developing a circumscribed persona, and found this increased as the materials one might work with—the plot, the characters, the language—were further limited. The game-like aspect of composing, the conscious delight in solving arbitrary problems of a size you can handle and discuss, stimulated imagination and decreased personal anxiety.

I usually emphasize one particular form in class discussion at particular times during the semester, and encourage each student to try out that form during the term. But I don't twist arms. Small exercises in class can provide all the students with some practice in the less exotic forms of exposition and argument. And if they become good narrators, describers, or dramatists in the course of a single semester, that's better than having them become grumpy or cliché-ridden essayists and disclaimers.

I no longer feel guilty for not explicitly dealing in class with the four levels of discourse, or the eight ways to organize an expository theme, or the difference between restrictive and nonrestrictive modifiers, or afraid of becoming frustrated by trying to make sure the students get the historical and literary pinups to go with the readings. I have actually come to enjoy reading students' essays, each of which is different, and, good or bad, stimulates my own imagination as possible material for future classes. I've even done some of my own assignments for fun!

I don't pretend this is a new approach, or even unique; I think it occurs to us all at times. It's just a matter of getting over feeling guilty or suspicious about consciously using an approach that's so personally enjoyable. Below is a sample exercise that utilizes this idea.

**Sample Exercise**
Read John Updike's 30-line poem "Ex-Basketball Player."

Updike himself transposed characters, theme, plot, imagery from one medium to another as a skilled "professional amateur" (as he liked to view himself). His poem "Ex-Basketball Player" was reworked five times—twice as a novel and three times as a short story.

Following Updike's example and practice, look at the images, characters, setting, and facts for possible plot development in the poem as providing material for compositions of various types. Notice how the nature of each medium or form of discourse demands that different elements of Flick's experience be emphasized; how your own experiences and responses to life and language transmute the elements provided in Updike's poem.

Below are some suggestions for this assignment. Remember to utilize what we have discussed about each particular form.

These are only suggestions—you may develop your own narrative, description, skit, exposition, or argument that takes off from

the experience of the poem.
1   Narrative
    a   First person—Compose a monolog by Flick at work, or
        taking his coffee break, or telling someone of his past vic-
        tories.
    b   Second person—Catch the waitress telling someone (girl
        friend, customer) about Flick.
    c   Third person—Tell the story using basically the same
        point of view as in the poem.
    You may use dialogue in any of these and may extrapolate
    from the incidents in the poem.
2   Description
    Describe the diner, the town, the gas station, Flick, Mae—or
    any combination of the above from a stranger's point of view.
3   Drama
    Use the character of Flick as described in the poem, and have
    him talk to the present high school "star," or with an old
    classmate who is now a successful businessman, or with his
    boss, or Mae.
4   Interview
    Interview Flick for the sports page of your high school news-
    paper on the occasion of his class's 10th Year Reunion.
5   Expository Essay
    a   A character in one of Updike's novels who is very like
        Flick says, "I once played a game very well. I really did.
        And after you're first-rate at something no matter what, it
        kind of takes the kick out of being second-rate." Write an
        essay in which you explain why you agree or disagree
        with this point of view. You may support your ideas with
        specific references to "Ex-Basketball Player" as well as
        your own experience.
    b   Compare the ideas on early success presented in
        Updike's poem with Housman's "To An Athlete Dying
        Young."
    c   Define "success" using the experiences and values ex-
        pressed in Updike's poem, supplementing them (or con-
        tradicting them) with your own experience.
6   Argument
    a   Prepare a deductive argument proving that "Living in the
        past will only lead to unhappiness."

b   Argue the point that high school curriculums foster competition without teaching skills or sophisticating the
student's values.

# Dear Ann:
# I Have a Problem

Albert C. Yoder

*Students can make dramatic some imagined (or real) human problems
and let classmates furnish suitable answers. Or the letters may voice
the woes of literary characters as they, rather than their authors, see
their problems.*

Discovering relevant, interesting and educationally worthwhile
writing assignments is a perennial challenge to the English instructor. I would like to suggest a simple exercise that meets
these criteria and is applicable to students of all ages.

This exercise has a number of variations, but all are based on the
advice columns found in nearly every newspaper. In fact, it might
be helpful if you had your students examine a few of these columns to see just how they are written. The exercise is simply
this: every student in the class is asked to draft a letter containing a personal problem, real or imagined, to a columnist. After
this is accomplished, the students are asked to randomly exchange their letters and compose suitable replies as if they were
now the columnist. The letters may be continually exchanged, so
that several students reply to any given letter. Since some of the
students may choose to discuss their own personal problems,
they should be encouraged to sign their problem letters in the
shorthand commonly found in the newspaper columns: Miser-
able in Memphis, Lonely in Loredo, Angry in Augusta. Finally, after the replies have been written, they may be returned to the student who posed the problem.

There are a number of variations on this exercise. Rather than
have the students formulate the problem the teacher can always
bring one and ask everyone to compose a reply to it. The replies
can then be read aloud and discussed. It may be helpful to begin
in this way and, then, after they have practiced composing solu-

tions, ask them to compose both a problem and a solution. But, if the teacher does supply the problem, he or she should probably secure it from a professionally written column. Advice columns are written for nearly every age imaginable and questions posed to these columnists will generally be more realistic than any the teacher could invent.

Students of all ages find this exercise relevant, interesting and challenging because the problems are theirs or are intimately related to their lifestyles. It maintains some continuity between what they do in school and their experiences outside it. The exercise is educationally worthwhile because it requires the students to formulate verbally both problems and solutions—no easy task. The problems and solutions can also generate almost endless, although profitable, class discussion involving moral discriminations and judgments of value.

This exercise is worthwhile for several other reasons. It provokes students to write because it creates a dramatic situation. It encourages students to write naturally in their own voices, rather than in stilted impersonal ones. And it forces the student to keep the audience in mind. Since peers will be reading both the problem and solution, the student becomes aware of the fact that writing is a public utterance.

A rewarding follow-up variation is to write the problems of literary figures as they might see their own situations, not always quite as their author presents them. Let Hester Prynne, Bartleby the Scrivener (or formerly inarticulate Billy Budd), Chaucer's Prioress, Pamela's Mr. —————, Polyphemus, Uriah Heep, Pope's Atticus and others voice their problems. Finally, students will gain a new appreciation of selectivity and control of nuance in the dramatic monologue as Tennyson, Browning, and others create it.

# DESCRIPTION

Experienced teachers need not be told again that one of the best ways of learning observation, effective verbal response, and control of style and tone is through the process of description. Here, psychologically, is an area where the writing teacher can reach some kind of success with almost all students, not just those who have already begun to catch on to the techniques of efficient organization or analysis. Relative success in a descriptive assignment may well be for many students the first stage in overcoming reluctance to write, in overcoming memories of earlier frustrating experiences in composition.

# Describing a Face

Alfred L. Crabb, Jr.

*Everyone knows what a human face is like, but few realize how much or how little of it can be conveyed by words until they've tried a word portrait. Mr. Crabb submitted this assignment from the University of Kentucky, Lexington, Kentucky.*

## Author's Comment

This exercise functions well early in the first semester for two reasons: it is relatively short, and it emphasizes a basic idea—that close inspection of a subject will reveal that there is a lot to say about it. The assignment can be successfully completed in 300 to 400 words, sometimes less; a few students discover that they must ration their words instead of padding. The assignment requires some organization, but it does not have to be based on an outline, and so it may precede the outline in the course.

Describe a person's face. This exercise may be based on any available materials, but *Time* covers work nicely. The system described here requires one more cover than the number of students in class.

## Step One

First, a cover is shown to the class. If it can be projected on a screen, so much the better. The members of the class are then asked how they would describe the person, ignoring completely the symbolic backgrounds or any special information they might have about the person. At first the comments will come at random, and these can be accumulated on the blackboard. Before long, a few questions will be necessary to draw out points that have not been covered. Such problems as how to describe the eyes: the eyebrows, the eyelashes, the eyelids, the whites, the irises, the pupils, the over-all eye shape, the placement on the head, the width, the size, the shadows, the wrinkles and creases, all these emphasize the necessity for accuracy, clarity, and completeness. At first the comments should be objective recordings of the facts before the class. Later, when the accumulated data begin to warrant it, problems in how to transmit this information effectively are introduced. Soon similes and parallels will be suggested, and different ways of describing a single feature will permit discussion of which is the most effective. Problems in organization arise: Is it better to give over-all impressions first, beginning with outstanding features, or is it better to work from top to bottom? Should everything about the eyes be told at the same time, or is some of the material unnecessary, or should the wrinkles be handled with other facial wrinkles? After this open discussion, the class is asked to write the description to be handed in at the next meeting.

These papers are in some degree the result of group composition and active teacher guidance, and yet they will vary widely. Comments by the teacher on each paper are a necessity, though grades might well be omitted. Skipping this whole step by having the class do its first writing on Step Two doesn't seem to work, however.

**Step Two**
Next a separate *Time* cover is given to each student. Again the students are warned to omit the background of the cover, and any private knowledge about the subject; they are reminded that an essential of the job is to discover an effective way to enable someone else to visualize the person they are describing. The cover is to be returned with the completed paper.

**Step Three**
An opaque projector can add an additional and valuable step at this point. Project a cover and read the paper that goes with it, or read a paper and then show the cover. Either way gives opportunity for additional insight into the problem and for judgment of how well it was handled by the student.

# Perceiving Resemblances

Sally Appleton

*Sometimes unfolding the whole realm of analogy with its infinite figurative possibilities is just a matter of calling attention to these possibilities in an orderly manner. Ms. Appleton sent this from Ohio State University, Columbus, Ohio.*

## Author's Comment

These three exercises aim to waken the student to the resemblances in their world—between things and things, between things and themselves. The exercise will encourage them to see in their early experience with poetry, that the exploratory and figurative language of poetry is not strange, but rather in harmony with their own perceptions. It will also use their ability to compare.

I   Ask the students, for a short outside class assignment, to compare themselves to one of the four elements, earth, air, fire, or water.

II   For a second outside class assignment, ask them to compare themselves with something which is part of the natural or mechanical world—a coffee pot, a bird, a garden, a desert. The fewer suggestions given by the teacher, the better this assignment works. The independent choice and explanation by the students will tell you a great deal about them as people. This exercise can be used as a basis for prescribing what poems to give them at first—those most natural to them, and those for which they need to have their awareness broadened.

III   The Hand: in-class assignment. This exercise is more disciplined and closely controlled than the other two, and should be performed step by step.

A   First, have each student decide what his or her hand resembles. It doesn't matter what position the hand is in when the student studies it, or what aspect of it he or she chooses to compare with another thing. (The specific kinds of comparison which follow will teach the students how they looked at their hands the first time, and whether they conceive of their hands as a power, or shape, or contact.)

B   Then have the students compare their hands to some other thing in the following specific ways: first, the structure of the hand; then its function or use; then its color; then its texture. Try to leave the way open for all possible resemblances they might see, by not suggesting too much and therefore limiting the originality or direction of their vision.

C   When the papers come in, assemble all the resemblances under their proper headings (THE HAND: *General, Structure, Use, Color, Texture*) on one sheet and give the students the results. By reading through the results together in class, the students will discover the possibility of many resemblances, and that the variety of resemblances relate to the variety of points of view. Most important, the exercise can be used to discuss the student's own attitude toward the body, its relationship to the world, and its important place in the making of poetry.

**Results from One Freshman Class**

SIMILARITY AND RESEMBLANCE: THE HUMAN HAND

**General**

Map, street map of city, structure of city, country; sign post; piston, remote control hooks that are my slaves, machine, crane, clam shovel, pliers; raccoon's paw, monkey's paw, nutcracker, dead branch, monster, Buck Eye wiener, rivers flowing into a body of water, rivulets, a leaf, pipes of pipe organ, animal's foot, falcon's claw.

A   *Structure:* Street map, structure of a city; flexible tool, scoop or shovel, rake, clam shovel, remote control, fork, useful machine with an imperfect part; thick sheet of rubber, Indian war bonnet, beam work, octopus, robot hand, spokes of a wheel, pipe organ; tree, leaf, tree branch, young stem.

B   *Use:* Derrick; machine which sorts, puts together, takes apart; hydraulic crane, steam shovel, mover for radioactive material, hammer to hit others, broom, club, rope, packing machine, scoop or pin setter for bowling, limbs of a tree, monkey paw, monkey tail; a press, claw, antenna of insect or dog's nose, the grip of tires.

C   *Color:* Oranges, light peach, rosy evening horizon, the sculptured object (an imitation sculptured peach made of pink translucent marble), multipurpose grease, sand, face powder, body color, old pine boards, wood, manila filing folder, light colored wiener, white house needing paint, blackboard eraser, plaster.

D  *Texture:* Fine wall paper, warmed wall paper cleaner, squeezing a rubber ball, foam rubber, harder than an egg, soft plastic, sealed plastic bag full of butter, overripe tomato, carrots, ripe peach, soft putty, animal skins, kipskin, cleaned rear leg of rabbit.

# On Being Specific

Barbara Paul

*Ms. Paul's "gimmick" arouses and allays the whole class, as Aristotle would have approved; the specificity is here combined with "the shock of recognition" to the advantage of future essays. This exercise was used at Berry College, Mount Berry, Georgia.*

I have found nothing so unspecific to younger writers as the phrase "specific words." Any forced composition is bound to be comprised of labored-over sentence fragments that say precisely nothing. So in an attempt to show my students at least what they were failing to produce, I devised the following exercise.

For a theme to be written in class I told the students to describe the personality and appearance of one of their classmates. Personal background, field of study, activities—all these were taboo; only physical description and character analysis would be accepted. The "gimmick" was that all this was to be done without mentioning the name of the person being described. After the students completed the theme, they were to write at the bottom of the last page the name of the one whose word portrait they had been endeavoring to paint for the last fifty minutes. After I had graded the papers, I had the students themselves unconsciously determine which were the themes that best employed specific words. I asked the class to stand, and as I read a paper, the students sat down as soon as they heard a description that did not apply to them. If the theme were a good one, there would be only one student standing by the time I finished reading the paper.

After the initial excitement of hearing themselves described wore off, the students settled down to listening for specific descriptive passages. They were quick to notice omissions and equally quick to recognize the value of any particularly well-turned phrase. Performing this assignment for the second time produced vastly improved descriptions with remarkably little repetition of either words or methods used the first time.

# The Reader's Perception: Implications through Word Order

William R. Slothower

*This subtle and eye-opening assignment demonstrates how the whole is more than the sum of its parts and depends on what order one meets the parts in. Mr. Slothower teaches at San Jose State University, San Jose, California.*

### Author's Comment
This exercise is based on Solomon Asch's studies of perception and the ways in which people organize their experience, as reported in his *Social Psychology*. (A detailed description of the procedure on which this exercise is based may be found on pages 208-220.) Several of Asch's experiments are easily adaptable to a composition assignment where the instructor wishes to give some attention to matters of semantics or to general philosophical problems concerning the relationship between language and human behavior. A feature of the exercise described below is that it can be used for a number of different purposes and that it can promote thinking and discussion on various aspects of language at a level that avoids getting involved in either the technicalities of semantics or the psychology of perception.

### Preparation for the Assignment
The only materials required for this assignment are sufficient lists of six adjectives to supply the whole class, arranged so that on half the lists, the order of the adjectives is reversed. The following adjectives, adapted from Asch, seem to work well:

*List A*　intelligent, industrious, impulsive, critical, determined, cold.

*List B*　cold, determined, critical, impulsive, industrious, intelligent.

## Procedure

Each student in the class is given one of the lists, which are distributed so that approximately one-half the members of the class have *List A* and the remainder have *List B.* Students are instructed to write a description of the kind of individual suggested to them by the six adjectives on the piece of paper before them. Some care must be taken to camouflage the true purpose of the assignment, and particularly the fact that the adjectives are in reverse order on half of the papers. I usually brief the class somewhat as follows:

> "The object of this assignment is to demonstrate the extent to which people are capable of sizing up a person even when they know only a few descriptive qualities about him. On the sheet of paper before you are six adjectives that describe a certain person. In a few paragraphs, write a description of the kind of person you think this individual is. Do *not* try to describe a living, specific individual whom you may know, such as your Uncle Frank. Remember also that the six adjectives all apply to only one person, about whom you are to write. For purposes of this assignment, do not discuss your adjectives or your work with your classmates. Neither is it necessary to work out an outline. Simply jot down your idea of the kind of person who comes to mind as you look at these six adjectives."

## The Descriptions

When the papers are turned in, the reader will find two general types of individuals described, but with a definite pattern of difference between them. In general (although in a class of 25 or 30, some variations from these norms will occur), those students who wrote from *List A* will describe an able, positively-valued individual whose shortcomings, if mentioned at all, are regarded as not serious enough to overshadow his or her merits. *List B* descriptions, however, will tend to portray a person who is something of a "problem," who is not regarded highly, and whose abilities are hindered by shortcomings.

Specifically, in *List A* descriptions, "intelligent" is not only valued but also influences the connotations of other adjectives in the list: "impulsive," "determined," and even "critical" tend to take on positive overtones. More significant, *List A* writers tend to explain away or in some manner justify "cold" in their accounts. Students with *List A* write, "He really isn't cold, but only seems to be because his job requires it," or, "When you get to know him, he isn't really cold at all." On the other hand, *List B* writers generally describe a person in whom coldness is the dominant characteristic and is neither rationalized nor justified: "I don't like the way he treats his employees"; "This man is even cold and aloof in his relations with his own family." Finally, "intelligence" in *List B* descriptions takes on negative connotations of craftiness, shrewdness, or selfishness: "He uses other people for his own private ends"; "He is smart enough to get what he wants from people."

**Discussion of Results**
After the papers have been read and returned, the instructor may proceed with discussion in any one of several ways. One approach is to begin by telling the class that while everyone had the same six adjectives, there were pronounced differences in the types of persons described. Ask two students who wrote contrasting descriptions (one from *List A* and one from *List B*) to read aloud their portraits. Following the reading, the instructor should call for discussion of differences between the descriptions of the two individuals and should help the class discover that the order of adjectives has been reversed. If this fact does not occur to the class, it should be revealed by the instructor at a strategic point in the discussion. At this time, the discussion may be directed by questions as to why the reverse order should make such a difference. Conclusions concerning the effect of word order and generalizations about the selection and sequence of adjectives in English are profitable.

# Describing Music *Itself*

Charles C. VanCleve

*After years of sensitivity to their own reactions to music, Mr. VanCleve of Centralia High School, Centralia, Illinois, challenges students to describe the music they are responding to, not the response.*

**First Session**
Prepare the class for the writing assignment by telling them that you are going to play a record for them. Inform them that they are to listen carefully to the music on the record, paying particular attention to the sounds that they actually hear. Although they may not like the music and, indeed, may not even consider it music, they are to concentrate on what happens and the order in which it happens. Tell them that you will play the record only once and that they may take notes as it is played. They are to write a theme describing what they have heard, the first draft of which will be due at the beginning of the next class session. Without commenting upon it, play George Antheil's *Ballet Mechanique.*

**Second Session**
Review the previous hour's assignment, emphasizing that it requires a description of the *music,* not the student's emotional reactions to, opinions about, or imaginative associations with the music. Then tell them you will play the record again for them, without benefit of class or teacher comments, and that they are to write a second draft making any desired revisions. The first draft will be turned in with the second draft at the beginning of the next session.

**Third Session**
Collect the papers at the beginning of the period, quickly picking out those first drafts which contain emotional reactions, expressions of opinion, or imaginative descriptions of what the music portrays to the student. Repeat the assignment, emphasizing once again that it requires a description of the *music.* Then read several of these papers to the class and let the students determine in what way each fails to follow the assignment. Continue the reading and discussion of the papers until the class clearly sees the differences between a description of the music (the sounds and the order in which they occur), a description of the associations and emotions the music produces in the mind of the listener, and the vague generalizations of a "turned off" mind ("It

stinks," "It's a mess," "It's stupid"). When these reactions to the assignment have been clarified, ask the students why anyone would react to the assignment in either of the last two ways. The roles played by inattention, both to the assignment and to the music, and lack of interest should be brought to the attention of the class. Some discussion of the attitudes which produce "turned off" reactions might also be beneficial at this point.

Next consider some of the second drafts which accomplish the assignment. These papers should be judged by the class on the basis of their clarity and whether or not the music is identifiable from their description. Comparisons between the relatively successful and unsuccessful papers should bring out the following points:

1   Vocabulary is important because it provides the means for the clearest, most concise mode of description.
2   A serious attitude on the part of writers is necessary for clear communication. If their attitude is not serious, their desire to communicate not strong enough, they will not take the trouble to relate the new experiences (sounds and patterns of sounds) to those with which they and their audience may be acquainted.
3   Hasty generalization and inaccurate thinking manifest themselves in the writers' choice of general terms in situations where more specific terms are within their grasp.
4   Some writers' familiarity with musical instruments and conventions allows them to actually perceive and note more than those writers who have not had such experiences. The same holds for any type of experience for which a description might be required. Aside from the fact that having a good vocabulary on a subject implies some experience with that subject, the vocabulary itself influences the range and fineness of our perceptions; distinctions are easier to note when one knows words which may be used to make these distinctions.
5   The vocabulary of value judgments makes them totally inadequate as vehicles for actually describing the music itself; these words and statements tell us *nothing* but the feelings or state of mind of the writer.

**Comments**
Although other similar musical works may be used, I have found George Antheil's *Ballet Mechanique* especially effective for sev-

eral reasons. The obscurity of the work makes it most unlikely that any of the students are already acquainted with it. Its unconventional instruments (woodblock, large and small airplane propellers, and large and small electric bells) force the student to search for descriptive phrases which will classify their sounds by drawing analogies with more familiar instruments and noisemakers. The conventional instruments (drums, pianos, xylophones, etc.) provide something recognizable for students who might otherwise be unable to produce anything intelligent about the music because they perceive nothing familiar enough to provide a starting place; most of these students are stayed from an immediate conclusion that the music is completely foreign to their experience and therefore too "far out" to merit any serious consideration. The *Ballet's* emphasis on rhythm rather than tonal pattern makes it a drastically new experience to most students. This newness creates most of the difficulties they encounter in perceiving it, but in so doing creates the problems which are necessary to make the *Ballet* a challenging object for an exercise in description.

# Picture to Word to Picture

Rosalie Webb

*This graphic demonstration of the need for precision combines the literary with the visual for maximum teaching effectiveness. Ms. Webb is a Regional Helping English Teacher in Arlington, Virginia.*

### Preparation for the Exercise
1   Locate an art teacher to collaborate with you and your class on an interesting Art/English experiment.
2   Find an abstract painting unfamiliar to the English students.
3   Display the painting in the front of the room.

### Exercise
As the students enter the room, ask them to write a detailed, specific description of the painting they see on exhibit. Instead of placing their names on their papers, ask them to use assigned numbers for identification later. After you have collected the descriptions, give them to the art instructor, who allows art students to select at random a paper. From the prose description,

they draw and paint the picture, also identifying their work by the same number as the composition and not by name. So that they can be matched later, the art teacher must maintain a record of their numbers. Each teacher should try to avoid much explanation as to the "why's and wherefore's" in order to create an air of mystery in what the students are doing, but each instructor should emphasize the necessity for specificity in both the descriptions and the painting.

**Follow-Up or Result**
Both teachers should arrange for a joint meeting of the classes with the original painting exhibited. This can be done in a place such as the cafeteria. The two numbers of prose descriptions and art work can be matched and placed together on tables before the classes arrive. Then the fun begins as the students enter and find their work and collaborating partner.

"That's not what I meant!"

"You did not follow my instructions!"

"Well, why didn't you say so?"

**Author's Comment**
The above students' comments teach the concept. The students have fun as they realize the importance of writing accurately, making the correct word choice, and giving specific instructions, and they see the need for following those directions precisely.

# Describing Geometric Forms for Feedback

T. J. Ray

*Mr. Ray of the University of Mississippi shows the need for precision and the need to keep the recipient's possible confusions in mind as one tries to communicate even with geometric exactness.*

Doldrums occur most often after midterm tests or after holidays or just when Spring is springing. At such times students display a marked lack of enthusiasm for the regular pursuits of composition. Teachers are not immune to this malady. It is then that a blow must be struck while the iron is cold. A successful exercise is a figure-description project which requires no preclass work on the student's part and need not extend beyond the class period.

At the beginning of class each student gets a numbered sheet with a figure drawn on it. The figures vary in complexity, although any one can be described in about forty minutes. The students describe the figures on their sheets, using only words and making no graphic notations to aid the reader. They may, of course, suggest objects that will help the reader to visualize the figure. One student described a skewed letter Z as a bolt of lightning.

When all the students are finished with their writing, the figures are collected, and the descriptions are distributed along with blank paper. The second student is asked to read the description carefully and redraw the figure on the blank sheet. When this step has been completed and all papers are returned, the original drawings are compared with student versions. Usually each pair will be similar enough so that it is clear that the description was accurate. When there is an obvious disparity, the teacher reads the description to determine which student is in error, the one who wrote the paper or the one who read it. Or the teacher can reproduce the figure on the blackboard as he or she reads the paper.

After this exercise students are better prepared to write other descriptions because they are convinced of the value of careful cataloging of details. Exercises of this type teach students to respect both detail and its arrangement; and they learn to deal with proportion and—if you go on to work with photographs—perspective as well. Such class projects also afford the teacher the opportunity to have the class write more without an increase in grading demands.

### Handout for Students
After you have read this, you will be given a sheet of white paper containing a design of some sort. After considering your drawing for some time, you are to write a description of what is on your paper. Do not worry too much about exact lengths of lines or degrees of angles. Your verbal description of the figure will then be given to someone else in the class with a clean sheet of paper. If your description is at all accurate, he or she should be able to reproduce a general image of what was on your original sheet. The test of suc-

cess for your description will be a comparison of the two figures. For that reason, please put the number of your drawing
on the outside of your description with your name. Do not include the number in your description. DO NOT MAKE ANY
MARKS ON THE SHEET YOU ARE GIVEN.

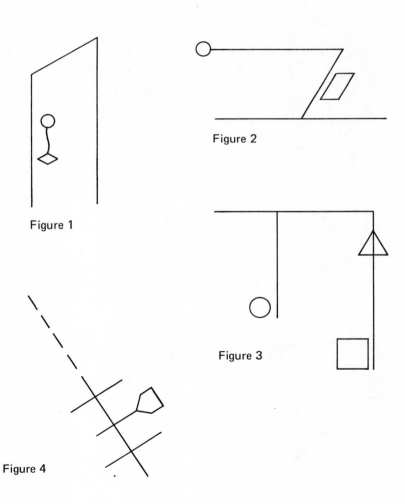

Figure 1

Figure 2

Figure 3

Figure 4

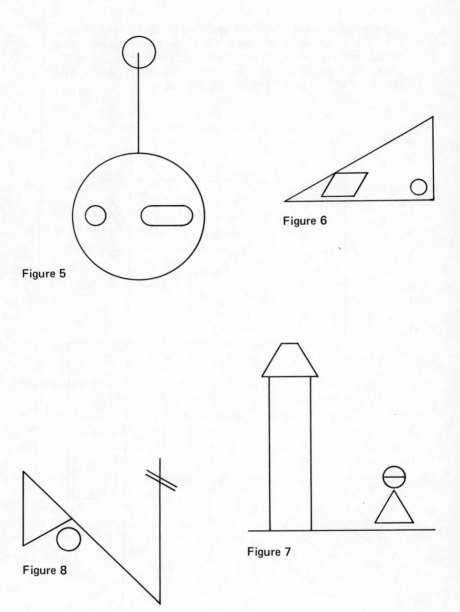

Figure 5

Figure 6

Figure 7

Figure 8

# Description: The Dominant Impression

Donald M. Murray

*Out of many possible impressions springing from the sensed details of a scene, students must train themselves to focus on one attitude that dominates all others. Thus the final prose picture is firmly based on concrete details, but not on all the concrete details. Mr. Murray teaches at the University of New Hampshire, Durham, New Hampshire.*

When students write descriptions, they often merely compile an inventory, listing everything from left to right or top to bottom. Writers are not interested in cataloging, but in recreating. They select and reject, report and ignore, even distort to achieve their truth. Most of the time they organize their vision around a dominant impression.

The concept of a dominant impression is simple but it is not obvious to most beginning students. Once students understand the importance of the dominant impression and learn how to utilize it, their descriptions—and often all their writing—will begin to develop force, clarity, and grace. Their paragraphs will begin to have both purpose and shape.

Writers begin with an abundance of information, but they should end only with that which is significant. Writing is thinking, the making of tough decisions, for writers have to decide what is most important and then communicate it to their readers. When writers describe, they have to cut away the unimportant from the important and leave standing the dominant impression they wish to communicate to the reader. It may help the students to think of a camera dollying in, pulling back, working with light and shadow, zooming in and out of focus. Writers, with their camera eye, decide (often through writing, not before writing) what it is they want to say. Once they know or feel the dominant impression, then they begin to command their material.

Let us see how this works by listing a few of the abundance of specific details a person might collect while waiting alone in a hospital emergency floor examining room.

1   bright ceiling light
2   hiss of door shutting
3   white tile walls
4   stainless steel tree on wheels
5   half-empty, upside-down bottle hung from tree
6   tube snaked over tree arm
7   bottle half filled with blood
8   stainless steel cart
9   tray on cart
10  hypodermic needles on tray
11  kidney-shaped stain-less steel receptacle
12  a bouquet of knives and scissors stick-ing out of a dish on the tray
13  a stainless steel box next to the wall
14  a trace of steam rising out of the box
15  barred ceiling vents
16  a revolving blue light outside the window
17  smell of ether
18  cold, black plastic floor
19  black examining table in the center of the room
20  a roll of paper at the top of the table
21  a great eye of a lamp leaning over the table
22  a sign on the wall, "Danger, Do Not Smoke"
23  a tall tank
24  a mask hanging giddily over its dials
25  somebody running by the door
26  a white cloth screen
27  a neat cigarette hole in one of the panels
28  a stainless steel piano stool
29  a left shoe
30  a stainless steel gar-bage can with a pedal to operate the top
31  a bandage half sticking out of the can
32  brown blood on the bandage
33  a radiator hissing
34  a white painted cab-inet with a big block
35  a sink with a high, arching faucet
36  a stainless steel power saw
37  a big soap bottle above the sink
38  a stretcher on wheels pushed against the wall
39  two crutches criss-crossed on the stretcher
40  an open cabinet jammed full of bandages
41  a red wall telephone
42  a white light on the phone blinking off and on, off and on
43  two fingers reaching out of a box of dis-posable plastic gloves
44  a blood-pressure gauge with its own wheels
45  sign on cabinet, "Drugs, Keep Locked"

Writers, using all their senses, knowledge, memory, and imagination, don't have 45 items to choose from, but 450, or perhaps even 4500, specks and bits of impressions which they may find are significant and of which they may not even be conscious until they start to write. They are like an octopus of a wrestler, faced with dozens of ways to grab hold of a subject. They simply have to make arbitrary decisions. If a writer, for example, decides to emphasize the loneliness he or she felt in a room, then all the details which do not contribute to this feeling of loneliness fall away. The writer is left then to discover the natural order of the remaining details which may communicate the dominant impression of loneliness.

> The door hissed shut and the quiet, after the undulating pain of the siren, seemed soft, something you could almost touch. It wasn't quiet so much as an absence of sound, as the bright whiteness of the room was an absence of color. I was alone with gadgets, knives, and tubes, and pipes, and masks. Nothing human, just equipment. And then I saw the shoe, just one shoe, a right shoe, still tied.

The writer chose that way to try to show loneliness, but there are dozens of other ways to approach the same descriptive paragraph, each one organized around a dominant impression. Here are some of them:

**The Revealing Specific**
Everything in the room was designed to look professional—the impersonal table, the objective knives, the bright light, the clean walls. But then, not quite tucked away under its cover of stainless steel, was the bandage and the brown, faded blood.

**A Single Sense**
The air had probably been sprayed clean and was being sucked up through the grates at the top of the walls by a fan somewhere slowly turning. The room almost didn't have a smell; it was just the memory of a smell, the same ether smell which seemed to rise from my father when they let me into the Intensive Care ward, and he reached up over the crib side to grab my hand before he asked, "Was it cancer?"

**Foreground and Background**
I couldn't focus on anything in the room but that tall, thin, uncomfortable black examining table. It seemed as if it were

waiting for me, and if I hopped up and sat on it it would somehow pull me down and hold me. Once down on that table I
would be a turtle flipped back on its shell, helpless, a patient.

### Close-Up
If I'd thought about it I would probably have feared the
knives, the needles, the operating table, the one trace of
blood, the great eye of the examining light. But now, left
alone, I found I couldn't stop looking at the red wall telephone and the silent ringing of the small yellow light, off-on,
off-on, off-on. Someone calling and no one answering.

### Documentation
The room was cold. Chill steel, cool tile, bloodless plastic
tubes and clear glass bottles, even the blue light from the po-
lice car drifting across the window was cool, coming and
going.

### Growing Awareness
I crouched down on the silly little stool and glanced almost
casually around the room, a stretcher, some crutches, a sink,
an examining table, a stainless steel scarecrow hung with a
bottle half-full of ketchup, a tray with three needles, and then
stuck in a jar, a bouquet of scissors and knives, ready for use.
Then, unable to look away from the neat precision of one curved blade, I began to believe the accident.

### Tone
Sitting, waiting, I tried to keep my mind in this one room.
Later there would be time to think about what happened and
might not have happened. And soon those steps passing by
the door would stop, and I would have to do what had to be
done then. But now I would concentrate on this room, this
bright room of tile and stainless steel, where there were no
shadows.

These examples obviously comprise a crude and artificial exercise. You can make up alternatives of your own—the startling sta-
tistic, the ironic twist, the change of pace, the impressionistic
vision—your own categories and your own examples. Such finger
exercises show beginning writers a few of the hundreds of alternatives available for writing a simple paragraph of description.
Remember that writers, however, don't click through each alter-
native in some computer in their brains, and they certainly don't
consciously select a pattern of development and then follow a
blueprint to write their description. Students shouldn't concen-

trate on models but on their subject. Writers don't look at a rhetoric of description when they sit down to write; they don't reach blindly into a grab bag of craft and neither should students. Writers look with their minds' eye at what they want to describe. They write and rewrite until their subject comes clear. They hone their words to reveal what is most important, what the reader should know or feel. Their purpose is nothing more—and nothing less—than trying to capture truth. And the dominant impression is but one device they may use to trap a truth and deliver it to the reader.

## RESEARCH

With no pretense of covering the broad topic of research, the exercises here nevertheless touch on central problems—how to handle borrowings, how to arrange material, how to deal with conflicting opinions, how to cope with history and change.

# Citing Borrowed Material

Katherine Burton

*Based on the principle of working from the familiar to the unfamiliar, Ms. Burton's assignment tackles the delicate problems of quotations direct and indirect, paraphrase, and fairness in interpretation. Ms. Burton used this exercise at Wheaton College, Norton, Massachusetts.*

## Author's Comment
Since students unversed in research often use the words of a source without acknowledgment when they have no intention of plagiarizing, I base an exercise on a single short passage which is before us all, preferably a passage with which we are all so familiar that even a single word from the source rings a bell in our minds. The students at first think that there is nothing new to be said about such a passage, but the range in their results shows them the infinite possibilities in paraphrase and comment.

## Exercise
1   Hand out duplicated slips containing the last sentence of Lincoln's Gettysburg Address:

> It is rather for us to be here dedicated to the great task remaining before us—that from these honored dead we take increased devotion to that cause for which they gave the last full measure of devotion; that we here highly resolve that these dead shall not have died in vain; that this nation, under God, shall have a new birth of freedom; and that government of the people, by the people, for the people, shall not perish from the earth.

2   Discuss the importance of quoting exactly, checking back to the source, what paraphrasing is, etc. Read a loose paraphrase in class too quickly for the sample to stay fixed in the students' minds:

> Lincoln concluded by pointing out the necessity of the dedication of the people rather than of the place. He reminded his hearers that the dead whom they honored had given full final devotion to a cause; the survivors should not do less, but should resolve firmly that the freedom for which the soldiers had died should be maintained in a people's government, a kind of government—he implied—in danger of perishing unless saved by firm resolution.

3   Ask students to write their own paraphrases with suitable acknowledgment of Lincoln's contribution to what they produce. Calling on various students to read their passages aloud will lead to as much discussion as desired on whether certain points made in the paraphrases are actually there in the original passage.

4   The isolation of particular points, using Lincoln's own words, is relatively easy. The students may call them out in quick succession instead of writing them down: "As Lincoln realized, the great task still remained." This leads to the point that it may still be necessary to acknowledge his paraphrasing even though a passage is fairly far removed from the source. We paused for the class to write samples:

> Lincoln never forgot that the nation, much as it had accomplished by its own efforts in a terrible struggle, was still a nation under God, that it should not be cocksure and irreligious, but even in its high idealism must remember that it was only under God that its high hopes were to be fulfilled.

> The conception of democratic government which Lincoln set forth was of a people's government of, by, and for the people, as his rhetorical phrases made so emphatic.

> As Lincoln implied in the conclusion to his Gettysburg Address, American democracy was the one great free government of the nineteenth century. If democracy failed here, it perished from the whole earth, he said in his final words.

This section in which only part of the material in the passage is used gives the teacher a chance to discuss relevancy as well as the differences between "said" and "implied" (for instance) and the whole matter of fairness to the source. But the teacher will have to watch the clock to get through No. 5 in the first class hour.

5   Students should be asked next to make single points in their own words:

> As Lincoln points out, the dedication was not to be of the place, but of the people who came to view it.

> Lincoln knew well that the place would lose its importance if it didn't inspire the people.

> Lincoln set up the dead as an inspiration to the devotion of the people.

6 The preceding exercises have built up to assigning a completely independent comment on the passage to be done before the next class hour. If any quotation or paraphrase is used, it should be subordinated to thought of the students' own. Discussion of results led to the matter of being true to the spirit of the original. We talked about which was the better of the two following passages:

> Lincoln's turning of the dedication from the place to the people must have profoundly stirred his audience. Awed by the historic battlefield, they must have trembled to feel that the real importance was in themselves, not in the ground on which they stood. To use modern jargon, it was audience-participation of a sort all the more thrilling because it was utterly unexpected, and Lincoln had proved himself a great master of ceremonies, all the greater in that he most certainly had no thought of himself as he stood there.

> Lincoln here seems to be attracted by the two themes of birth and death. He first dwells on the past, on those who died for their country; he presents the hopelessness of the feeling that perhaps they died in vain and implores the living to look to them and their actions for inspiration. Then he turns to birth, figuratively used, a new birth of freedom, a chance to start again, a new promise of hope for the country. Here is the goal to which the people may aspire. Death and the past, birth and the future—and those who are between them, in the present, must receive inspiration from the one and strive toward the other.

Comparison of the two passages brought up, incidentally, such questions as whether the speech was, in fact, well received, whether the war was over at the time the speech was made, what the occasion was, who was there (whether there had been special arrangements to bring relatives of those who had died there), etc. We didn't try to answer most of these questions, but left the matter at the general realization that to write even this short comment on a short familiar passage as well as possible would take some research, that it would easily grow into a miniature source theme, that most academic work does, and that this is why the source theme techniques are so much emphasized in English classes.

# Jigsaw Puzzle in Exposition

David Kerner

*While incidentally showing the difference between journalism and sober research, this exercise tests the students' abilities in assembling from scrambled material the causes, the resulting problem, and the possible solutions. Mr. Kerner sent this in from Pennsylvania State University, University Park, Pennsylvania.*

## Author's Comment

This exercise is a fifty-minute test of the upper freshman's ability to write a research paper: the student is required to (1) construct an expository composition from moderately disassembled facts and (2) present these facts in plain English undeflected by the wording in the source(s) of information; the student's interest in finding facts is not tested. Typical errors of construction and wording are listed in Appendix B. Comparison of Appendixes A and C reveals differences in method between unadulterated exposition (or "unleavened"?) and journalism which entertains and persuades better than it informs.

## Directions

Rearrange the following jumbled information in an expository composition intended to inform a reader who knows nothing of the subject. Note that the facts within each numbered paragraph do not necessarily belong together. Eliminate wordiness, attempts at wit, and bias, but omit no facts. *Use your own words as much as possible.* Assume that you are writing at the time the account was reported.

1  Trouble came last year in Argentina. Grain and cattle production slumped after Peron had increased taxes on farmers. Exports of beef were slashed, but Argentines still got their first taste of a meat shortage.
2  Peron has since eased up on cattlemen, but the supply of beef still doesn't meet the demand. Peron can't afford to lose the adoration of his carnivorous citizens.
3  In the busy center of Buenos Aires a "Health Cooking" stand features free recipes for tasty meals without meat. People hurrying by stop a minute to read the warnings on a tremendous blackboard above: the general idea is that if they eat too

much meat they invite troubles like gallstones and high blood pressure. This show was put on by the Minister of Health, Ramon Carrillo.

4   Of course, the reason for this hullabaloo is the beef shortage, which may or may not be as bad now as it was last year, when Buenos Aires restaurants were running meatless days, and lines waited in front of butcher shops.

5   An Argentine is used to eating 235 pounds of meat a year, most of it beef. Compare this to American consumption—130 pounds, about half of it beef. Just about no other country in the world consumes more meat per capita than Argentina. But even with this heavy home consumption, Argentina used to export plenty of beef.

6   Last week the government ran an educational conference called "Rational Eating." The government wants the people to "modify negative eating habits" and get healthier. When Carrillo spoke to 4000 citizens of the Republic of Beef, he got as excited as a Holy Roller gunning for converts: Eating meat can shorten your life! eat less meat and more vegetables! spread the good word!

7   Argentina needs to export beef to pay for necessary imports.

## APPENDIX A: INSTRUCTOR'S VERSION

Until recently, Argentines ate an average of 235 pounds of meat a year, mostly beef—perhaps the world's record (Americans eat 130 pounds, about half of it beef), and nevertheless exported enough beef to pay for necessary imports; lately a beef-cattle shortage has been threatening Argentina's economic stability and Peron's popularity.

Apparently because Peron had raised taxes on farmers, grain and cattle production slumped last year. Home demand slashed beef exports, but in Buenos Aires there were still meatless days in restaurants and lines outside butcher shops.

Peron has tried to encourage production, by lighter taxes on cattlemen—with little if any success. Now he is trying to discourage consumption, by anti-meat propaganda: last week, at a government-sponsored conference on "Rational Eating," Health Minister Ramon Carrillo warned 4000 delegates that since meat can shorten a man's life, Argentines should eat less meat and more vegetables; in midtown Buenos Aires, Carrillo has put up a huge blackboard warning that too much meat leads to gallstones and high blood pressure, while below, a "Health Cooking" stand hands out meatless recipes.

## APPENDIX B: STANDARDS
### Errors of Construction
Following the test's arrangement from paragraph 1 to 7 (even keeping the numbers); not joining 3 and 6; omission of an important point, such as the lowering of taxes; failing to separate the chronological material (the apparent cause, the result, the attempts at solution) from the logical (the explanation of the economic, social, and political importance of the high production of beef in Argentina), and failing to see that this explanatory background must come early, preferably in the first sentence; confusing the sequence of events (for example, making the lowered taxes the immediate consequence of the shortage, or blending the two calendar years mentioned, as in "beef exports were slashed and some taxes lowered"), or not presenting the sequence chronologically (many students keep the "organization" in 4, telling how bad last year's shortage was when they are writing about this year's shortage; they put the lowered taxes after the anti-meat campaign; they begin with the propaganda of the Ministry of Health, before the reader knows there is a shortage); failing to join the two atempts at solution, and failing to see the dovetailing of these attempts (raising production and lowering home consumption until the preshortage surplus is again available for export).

### Errors of Wording
General "echoing"—reliance on inadequate original wording ("eased up on cattlemen" in 2 should become "lowered taxes") or retention of wordiness ("recipes for tasty meals without meat" in 3 should become "meatless recipes"; "people hurrying by" in 3 should be omitted; etc.); innocent retention of the pun ("first taste of a meat shortage") and of the sarcastic tone ("carnivorous citizens," "Republic of Beef," "hullabaloo," "show"), including the misinterpretation of Carrillo's message at the end of 6 as direct discourse; lack of skepticism concerning both pro- and anti-Peron implications, as in taking for granted that the increased taxes were the sole cause of the shortage (if so, why did *their* cause(s) continue to be of more importance than their consequences?), or in failing to make the point (as opposed to echoing

it in the tone) that Peron is spreading what is probably propaganda, not information.

**Note**

That some of these *are* errors may seem open to debate; instructors who nevertheless see value in this kind of exercise should look for a short piece of exposition whose natural order is not wholly chronological or equally obvious. This kind of test cannot be both adequately useful and just if the material does not fall into that single logical, final arrangement—as predetermined as the piecing together of a manufactured jigsaw puzzle—which the good student should be encouraged to look for when writing exposition. Many students compose a paper as though stringing beads of one size and color—the paragraphs are interchangeable. Good students who are too busy or unwilling to find all the facts or ideas their research topic demands should see the corresponding holes in their composition as clearly as they would see the spaces for missing pieces in a jigsaw puzzle; besides, some of the pieces they have found may be isolated, their position undetermined. Proust, in *Swann's Way*, speaks of the artist as copying what exists already in a heaven of possibilities; the bad artist's eye or ear falters—and invents instead of copying what is there. Trying to find the truth is similar: a life-and-death search for the pieces and their places in a jigsaw puzzle which is whole, boundless, and endlessly shifting, like the river in *Life on the Mississippi*—the pieces have a habit of losing their shape or color, no longer fitting, after they have been placed. Is it grandiose to invoke Proust and truth in freshman composition? The question is big, too! Whom should it embarrass?

## APPENDIX C: ORIGINAL VERSION
**Argentina: Let Them Eat Vegetables**
Meat can shorten a man's life, warned Health Minister Ramon Carrillo last week in a speech to 4,000 fellow Argentines. With evangelistic fervor, Carrillo urged them to eat less meat and more vegetables, and to persuade other citizens of the Republic of Beef to do the same. The occasion was a government-sponsored conference on "Rational Eating." Officially, its purpose was to improve Argentines' health by educating them to "modify negative eating habits"; actually the conference was another effort to relieve Argentina's beef shortage.

By most countries' standards, Argentina has plenty of beef. But Argentines are just about the most carnivorous people on earth, stowing away an average of 235 lbs. of meat a year, mostly beef. (U.S. average: 130 lbs., about half of it beef.) Despite heavy home consumption, Argentina used to have lots of beef for export. Then Juan Peron & Co. began tinkering with the national economy. A soak-the-farmers policy cut heavily into grain and cattle production. Last year, despite severely curtailed beef exports, Buenos Aires got its first taste of a meat shortage, with meatless days in restaurants and queues outside butcher shops. Since then, Peron has given cattlemen a somewhat better break, but beef is still in short supply.

Peron's problem is to export more beef to pay for essential imports without making the beef-loving voters at home too unhappy. In the drive to bring down meat consumption, Health Minister Carrillo is trying to scare his countrymen into becoming vegetarians. At a busy corner in downtown Buenos Aires, he has put up a "Health Cooking" stand featuring free meatless recipes, and a huge blackboard warning of disorders, from gallstones to high blood pressure, which he insists are caused by excessive meat-eating.

**Copyright Time Inc. 1952**

# Controlled Source Research

Philip M. Griffith

*Matters of correct form mingle with problems of interpretation in this mini-research project by Philip Griffith, now of the University of Tulsa, Tulsa, Oklahoma.*

**Author's Comment**
In connection with the introduction, or review, of elementary research technique and documentation, the following exercise was devised and used many years before the now popular "controlled methods" approach was applied widely on the college freshman level. It may be assigned as a cooperative teacher-class project for classroom study, as an out-of-class assignment, or as an

hour's test in documentation. A standard English handbook or approved style sheet (preferably the *MLA Style Sheet*) should be utilized. Teachers should, of course, devise their own "model" paragraph and rigidly adhere to the recommended style of documentation. This exercise has the advantage of not exhausting student interest, often the disadvantage of a longer casebook assignment.

Suppose that your research paper is concerned with the early career of Andrew Jackson. You have assembled in your notes the following quotations, all of which treat the controversial problem of Jackson's birthplace.
1   Write the paragraph dealing with Jackson's birthplace, utilizing the materials below.
2   Document with correct footnotes. Observe that the sources given below are complete, but incorrectly arranged, punctuated, and capitalized.
3   Compile this part of the bibliography.

a   Chicago, lewis publishing company, 1941, Archibald henderson, volume II, *North Carolina, the old north state and the new,* pages 42-43.

> For many years Andrew Jackson believed and repeatedly stated that he was a native of South Carolina. For example, on August 11, 1824, in reply to a query as to the place of his birth, Jackson wrote to James H. Witherspoon of Lancaster, South Carolina: "I was born in South Carolina, as I have been told, at the plantation whereon James Crawford lived, about 1 mile from the Carolina road (crossing) of the Waxhaw creek...."

> James D. Craig in 1828 sent all the original affidavits (of those present at or having family-neighborhood knowledge of the birthplace of Jackson) to George Nevills of Ohio, chairman of a Jackson committee. These affidavits evidently came to Jackson's notice, and convinced him that he was born in the George McKemey house, present Union County, North Carolina, the exact spot being located by a boulder just 407 yards east of the eight-mile state line between North and South Carolina which runs due north and south.

b   *The life of andrew jackson,* new york, John spencer Bassett, Macmillan company, 1925, pages 5-6.

The exact spot at which Jackson was born has become a subject of controversy. By a tradition which lingered in the Leslie branch of the family the event was said to have occurred at the house of George McKemey. When the mother, so the story runs, journeyed from her abode to her sister's home, she stopped for a visit at the home of McKemey, and here labor came upon her. But when she was able to travel she continued her journey: and thus it came about that people thought the Crawford home welcomed into the world the future President.

c    Marquis James, 1938, *The Life of Andrew Jackson,* Bobbs-Merrill Company, New York, page 10.

Elizabeth (Jackson) and her boys slept that night at the home of one of Mrs. Jackson's sisters, one would think Jane Crawford, whose house was nearest by two miles and the best provided for the reception of guests. Before sunrise a few mornings later 'at the plantation whereon James Crawford lived . . . on the 15th of March in the year 1767,' Elizabeth Jackson's third son was born. Such is General Jackson's own Statement as to the place of his birth. In the opinion of the present reviewer it is the best evidence available bearing on the issue though several of his biographers have accepted an elaborate and interesting tradition that he was born at George McKemey's. In any event Elizabeth named the baby Andrew, carried him to be baptized in Waxhaw Church and took up her permanent abode under the Crawford roof.

d    Dictionary of American biography, Thomas P. Abernethy, volume IX, "Andrew Jackson," 1932, page 526.

JACKSON, ANDREW (Mar. 15, 1767—June 8, 1845), seventh president of the United States, was born in the lean backwoods settlement of the Waxhaw in South Carolina.

# The Movie Review
# As a First Step
# in Research

Edgar F. Daniels

*Exposure to a variety of opinions about a familiar medium is a good way of approaching objectivity in research for the beginning researcher. Mr. Daniels used this at Bowling Green State University, Bowling Green, Ohio.*

## Exercise
Students choose a movie, usually one that they admire. Then, through the *Reader's Guide, International Index, Filmfacts, Multi Media Reviews Index, Film Review Index, International Index to Multi-media Information,* or Stanley Kaufman's anthology, *American Film Criticism* (New York, 1972), they locate at least five reviews of this movie. Their job is now to compose a theme in which they sum up critical sentiment toward specific aspects of the picture, such as plot, directing, acting, photography, and ideas. If they wish, they may interpose their own opinion.

## Author's Comment
This assignment serves several purposes:
1   It provides a simplified and interesting introduction to research, without plunging students directly into the full-blown research paper.
2   It requires students to interpret relatively sophisticated commentary, discerning the evaluation implicit in sometimes figurative language.
3   It trains them in handling quotations. (I require that most of the ideas be in the students' own words, with only striking evaluative words quoted.)
4   It makes very obvious any defects of underdeveloped paragraphs, incoherence, lack of unity, and lack of topic statement.
5   It gives an opportunity to handle the problem of plagiarism in advance of the term paper and in a situation where it can be detected and traced much more easily than in the general research paper.
6   A required bibliography provides a modified introduction to this aspect of research and also aids the teacher in No. 5.

7   There is a final benefit that goes beyond the development of communicative skills. This assignment brings students into contact with literary tastes usually quite different from their own. Often they find their favorite movie or movie star disparaged, and their first reaction is angry disagreement. But encounters like this lead them to question their standards in the one art area where they have a vigorous interest.

# Doing Research on Words

Elmer F. Suderman

*This prototype assignment in word history is illuminating for neophytes. Students will astonish themselves at how much can be uncovered about a word and will learn some basic research techniques and attitudes at the same time. Mr. Suderman teaches at Gustavus Adolphus College, St. Peter, Minnesota.*

**Author's Comment**
The following topic was assigned after the class had read and discussed the selections on "Dictionaries, Words, and Meanings," and "The History of English" in Leonard F. Dean and Kenneth G. Wilson, *Essays on Language and Usage.* On the day on which the theme was announced the assignment was the reading of Stuart Robertson and Frederic C. Cassidy's "Changing Meaning and Values of Words." As the assignment was made, the period was spent not only in discussing the methods by which words change in meaning but also in reviewing the functions of the various dictionaries and the way in which English words have changed in spelling and pronunciation. Except for the material in brackets, I gave the students the following assignment.

Write a paper on "The History and Development of the Word *depot* and Its Meaning." Consider the spelling of the word and any changes that occurred when the word was borrowed from its original source and any changes that have occurred subsequently. Consider the pronunciation of the word and any changes that occurred when it was borrowed and any changes that have occurred subsequently. The word may well have different meanings. To indicate pronunciation, use the International Phonetic Alphabet. Finally, consider the development of the meanings of *depot.* Keep in mind that words can change in scope by speciali- zation and generalization [*depot* has undergone both] and in sta- tus by amelioration and pejoration [again *depot* exemplifies both processes]. A word may also change meaning by functional change: a noun, for example, may become a verb, a verb a noun, a noun an adjective, and so on. [*Depot* has changed from a noun to an adjective and to a verb since its introduction into English.] A word, furthermore, can acquire a slang usage and thus change in meaning. [There is no example of slang usage of *depot* unless *repple-depple* for *replacement depot* used in England during World War II can be cited.] Finally, a word may change in meaning by the addition of a prefix or a suffix, by internal change, by com- pounding [I have found no examples of these changes], or by be- coming a part of a combining word [as in *depot agent, depot wagon*, and the interesting *depot loafer*].

Since the meanings of words, spelling and pronunciation have changed at different rates of speed and in different ways in the United States than in England, it is necessary to consider differ- ences in the word in the two countries. The necessity of keeping chronology in mind should be obvious.

The following sources—not all of which will be relevant for the word *depot*—should be consulted in gathering material for this paper: *The Century Dictionary and Cyclopedia* (CDC); *The English Dialect Dictionary* (EDD); *Dictionary of Americanisms* (DA); *Dic- tionary of American English* (DAE); Skeat's *Etymological Diction- ary of the English Language* (EDEL); Samuel Johnson, *A Diction- ary of the English Language* (SJ); *Oxford English Dictionary* (OED) and Supplement (OEDS); *Webster's Dictionary of Synonyms* (WDS); *Webster's Third New International Dictionary* (WT), which should be compared with *Webster's New International Diction- ary,* Second Edition (WS), and if available, with the First Edition (1828). Simplify your citations by using the abbreviations used above. Complete as this list may seem to you, you may find other helpful sources: indeed some helpful sources have purposely been eliminated from this list for you to find. Do not, moreover, ignore your own observation and reading.

After you have collected the information, determine upon some basis of organization which will be clear to you and to the reader, and then write a paper presenting your findings as effectively and interestingly as possible.

**Further Comment**

Aside from the obvious advantage of allowing the teacher to exercise almost complete control over the material, the assignment has several other advantages. Knowing that the material we were discussing would have to be put to use in writing their weekly theme, the students entered more freely into the discussion, took more careful notes and asked more perceptive questions. The assignment requires the students actually to find and use the dictionaries in the library (no small achievement in itself) and to compare the different uses of various kinds of dictionaries. The exercise in the use of the library is not the least of the values of the topic. One student called it a second term paper.

It is unusual, yet highly desirable, to find a topic limited enough that the student can for once examine, if not all, then at least most of the available secondary material. On the other hand, it is a salutary experience for the student to discover that even the most restricted topic offers a wealth of material. Students can write five typewritten pages without much turgidity.

The assignment gives students an opportunity to check the dictionary against their own observations of the use of *depot,* although in my experience with the assignment not many students took advantage of this opportunity. No one, for example, talked to a depot agent to see what he thought of the status of the word or of the relative merits of *station master* or *depot agent.* No one looked through a daily newspaper or a railroad magazine to see how the word is used today. Perhaps another theme in which the students would be asked to make such firsthand observations would prove valuable. Some students did, however, make use of Bergen and Cornelia Evans, *A Dictionary of Contemporary American Usage,* and cite their discussion of *depot* and *station* and of the pejoration of *depot.* Others cited George Philip Krapp, *The English Language in America* and H. L. Mencken, *The American Language.* No student, however, found the rather lengthy discussion of *depot* in Albert H. Marckwardt, *American English.*

The assignment was an extremely effective way of teaching students the English habit of borrowing and the subsequent transformation of meaning. It is one thing to tell freshmen that words are constantly entering the language. It is another and far more forceful thing for them to look up *depot* in Johnson's *Dictionary* and find it missing. Had all of the printings of Webster's Unabridged been available, it would have been interesting to discover in what year Webster first defined *depot,* or, if more resources had been at hand, to compare the time *depot* was first entered in Worcester and Webster. The assignment, furthermore, gives the student firsthand observation of changes in meaning. It is one thing for students to write the definition of pejoration in their notebooks; it is quite another for them to see the process in the citations early in the twentieth century in the dictionaries and then to find evidence that the amelioration is taking place today.

To trace the development of the word *depot* gives the students some knowledge of the close connection between the social and cultural history of a nation and the development of its vocabulary.

Finally, the assignment forces the students to find ways of organizing relatively tractable, yet not the most exciting material in the world in a coherent, cogent, and effective way. It is incidentally worth noting that the organization of the papers which I felt should have been the most simple part of the assignment offers the greatest obstacle in the assignment.

The happy fact remains that there are several hundred thousand other words which are amenable to the same treatment. Among them in recent years, *trip, vulgar, drive,* and *aggression* have worked particularly well.

# THE SHORT STORY

While we all recognize there is creativity outside of fiction, for some students the imaginative flight of fancy furnished by writing short stories has particular satisfactions unavailable elsewhere. However, many of them find the middle portion of the narrative goes most easily, while the opening and closing sections cause agony, sweat, and (at least metaphorically) tears. It was Hemingway, no beginner in fiction, who was rumored to have rewritten the last page of *A Farewell to Arms* thirty-nine times. To help students over at least the initial hurdle in short-story writing, these three exercises may be useful.

# Point of View in Writing Short Stories

Herbert E. Arntson

*Mr. Arntson of Washington State University at Pullman, Washington, offers a fundamental prewriting exercise for authors of short stories in order to attain control of point of view and thus maintain narrative consistency.*

One could wish for less oversimplification, fewer arcane diagrams that need clarification, and less blurring of terminology in presentations of point of view. "Omniscience," for example, always appears in discussions of this basic matter, and often is handled without considering elements that may be included in it.

In treating the problem, I begin with the issues involved rather than with terms. I see these issues as three questions (in no special order) which the student should consider in arriving at a unified concept of his point of view:

1  What identity will be used as the point of viewing?
2  How objective or subjective will this viewing be?
3  What will be the person of the teller?

Will the author write and the reader know the story through the perception of a particular character (or a point beside that character)? Will that character reveal his or her thought and emotions, or merely observe? Will the story be told in the first, second, or third person?

Although we are inclined to offer injunctions concerning the answers, perhaps we should rather suggest the possibilities. Usually students choose either first or third person as narrator, and either author-character or character as identity of viewer. They often utilize this person's thoughts and feelings. That is, they usually limit themselves without any outside help. The point we should make is simply that writers should become aware of what they are doing and how they are revealing the story, so that the reader can know the avenues of telling and the writer can utilize these avenues with appropriate emphases.

Should the teacher insist on consistency? Certainly; but the fact that there are such things as multiple points of view, or a shifting point of view, or a "central intelligence" or ghostly viewer with considerable insight (omniscient viewer), and so on, should remind the student that consistency has the virtue of a kind of contract between writer and reader rather than the stigma of inhibiting rule. Faced with such choices, the student is likely to resolve the point-of-view problem with an eye to credibility.

# Getting a Short Story Under Way (I)

Cloyd Criswell

*This exercise makes sure the student will not flounder unduly over openers, having been given a beginning with several elements to synthesize—and a follow-up if it is needed. Mr. Criswell teaches creative writing at Lehigh University, Bethlehem, Pennsylvania.*

## Author's Comment

I have used this method several times, both with undergraduates and graduate students. I find that it stimulates discussion since the student identifies with the individual mentioned in the paper he or she is given.

The initial writing exercise extends over two class sessions. Students are given one of four situations from Group One, which is typed on the upper half of one sheet of paper. On the rest of the page they write in class in ten minutes an original sentence or two which explains and develops the guide situation. These papers are read, compared, discussed. The students are assigned the task of carrying this beginning through story form to a conclusion. If, by the following class session, any students have been unable to do the assignment—and many are not able—the second group of situations, each of which is a direct result of that situation first dealt with by the student, is given a ten minute treatment in class. The exercise can be continued in following sessions as long as the creativity of the teacher endures or until students learn to take raw materials and write them into something of a narrative. In no class is the student informed of the Group One exercise until the teacher is ready to issue the copy. The surprise element aids the students' use of imagination.

**Group 1**

A  You are caught in a snow storm on a street you know well, yet it seems strange to you. Night, cold flakes, dim lights. Why are you there?

Follow-up. From somewhere in the shadows steps a man. You do not know him. He asks a direction of you. You think of the answer you mean to give him, but you never give it. Why not?

B  You are standing at a crossroads in a farm region at high noon. Light, space, heat. Why are you there?

Follow-up. An approaching car comes to a stop. The driver recognizes you for someone else, gets angry when you do not accept his invitation to a place you do not know. In the stranger's opinion who are you? Where does he want to take you?

C  You sit on a wide window sill in an old, Victorian house. Something attracts your attention in the night outside the window. Why are you there?

Follow-up. The door to the room opens. Leaning against the frame is a man you have not expected, a friend once reported to have been killed. Where was his death supposed to have occurred?

D  You stand at a mountain stream in the early morning. The water, the sound hold your attention. Why are you there?

Follow-up. You are not far from your destination. You remove some of your clothing to refresh yourself in the water. Before you know it a stranger has come from nowhere and has your jacket in his hand. What is in its pockets?

# Getting the Short Story Under Way (II)

Laurence Perrine

*Boldly furnishing the basic plot and basic characterization, Mr. Perrine helps students focus their energies on telling the tale so that it will live. He teaches at Southern Methodist University, Dallas, Texas.*

### Author's Comment

The purpose of the assignment is (1) to provide an exercise in composition, (2) to sharpen perceptivity in reading through experience with the practical problems of short story writing. Most freshmen, if asked to write an original short story, waste so much time trying to think up a plot that they can hardly get started, and, when they do get started, their main emphasis is on narrating plot. By providing the plot, this assignment saves their time and forces them to concentrate on more important matters. Freshmen respond to the assignment by writing two or three times the 500 words normally required of them. Part II gives them the chance to compare their way of handling the problem with the original writer's, and thus further to increase their appreciation of good fiction. (The summarized stories have been chosen partly for brevity. They range in length from 670 to 1500 words.)

### Part I

A good short story need have only a very simple plot, as you have by now discovered. Given below are summaries of plots which four modern writers have used for effective stories. Choose one of them and write a brief story using it as basis. (Do not choose any of which you recognize the original.)

Remember your task is not merely to *tell* a tale, but to make it *live*. To do this, you must dramatize it—tell it through the human beings involved.

Before you begin, decide what point of view you intend to use; whether, if you use the point of view of a single character, that character should be a main character or an observer; and whether you will use the first person or the third. Decide how you will characterize your main characters, and how much use you can make of dialogue. Then go to it.

1   A henpecked, browbeaten, meek man drives his domineering wife to town, leaves her at the hairdresser's, parks his car, does some shopping, and meets his wife at the hotel. During this commonplace round of affairs, he finds an escape from reality in daydreams, compensating for his meekness and inferiority by imagining himself in various heroic roles.

2   A spoiled, self-indulgent woman, leaving a bridge party, decides to demand a regular allowance from her husband. Riding the crowded subway she notices the frayed overcoat of the man in front of her. Dramatizing its wearer, she decides he is a hard-working man who is having a hard time sending his children through school and who never spends money on himself. She feels quite sympathetic toward him.

    Back home, she finds her husband there before her. She feels dissatisfied with him: he seems so shabby and resigned. She asks him for a $50 monthly allowance. He hesitatingly agrees, but says he will not be able to begin it till next month. Then she notices her husband's overcoat: it is in the same condition as that of the man she had observed on the subway!

3   When she is four, a young girl is left an orphan by the death of her mother. She lives with relatives until she is thirteen, then becomes a lady's maid. During her service she becomes engaged to a young man in a florist's shop. On the day when he comes to take her to buy furniture, however, her lady is slightly ill. The maid suddenly realizes that she cannot bear to leave her lady, and she calls off the marriage.

4   A loyalist officer, reconnoitering a bridge and watching for advancing Fascist troops, finds an old man sitting by the road at a bridge. The old man had been warned to leave his little town—where he had kept two goats, a cat, and some pigeons—because of an expected artillery barrage. The loyalist officer tries to get the old man to move on, but the old man is too tired, too confused. He does not really understand the war.

**Part II (Assigned after Part I has been submitted)**
Listed below are the original stories based on the plots which you used for your stories. Find and read in the library the story which

uses the plot you used. Then make a list, in sentence form, of differences between the original author's treatment and yours, concentrating on those differences which make one story more effective than the other.

1 James Thurber, "The Secret Life of Walter Mitty"
2 Sally Benson, "The Overcoat"
3 Katherine Mansfield, "The Lady's Maid"
4 Ernest Hemingway, "Old Man at the Bridge"

Part II can be facilitated if the teacher distributes a bibliography of books in which these stories occur (with their call numbers), or if the books are placed on reserve.

# Rewriting

Skill in detecting and repairing blemishes can result from individual or class study of heavily-doctored passages containing a variety of common weaknesses. Visually or aurally, the staccato of a series of short sentences, the monotony of subject-verb-object, S-V-O, S-V-O, or the interminableness of an unfocused sentence can be seen and avoided. Similarly, students learn how to energize dead prose and compare their improvements with colorful, effective, original versions.

# An Exercise in Rewriting

George McFadden

*Sometimes students can be led to efficient rewriting by trying to clear up the ineptitudes of others. By varying the material, the teacher can match the degree of ineptitude to the needs of any particular class. Mr. McFadden now teaches at Temple University, Pittsburgh, Pennsylvania.*

## Author's Comment

I wish to overcome students' inability to revise their own writing—an inability partly due to fascination with their own text and partly to a fetish for neatness instilled during earlier school years. I had grown tired of watching freshmen smile complacently as they read over themes which I knew were crawling with errors.

We read Churchill's "Painting as a Pastime," and in the discussion emphasize the joy that comes from messing about with oil paints (or carpentry, or anything constructive). I read the class an advertisement telling how you can be an artist automatically with one of those "paint by numbers" kits. They never fail to laugh, showing that they recognize the difference between Churchill's creative joy in plastic manipulation and the mere mass-produced time killer. At this point they are ready for the exercise, a mimeographed paragraph which I have adapted from the favorite of freshman anthologies, "Farewell, My Lovely." In order to inspire the confidence which Churchill recommends, I have made my paragraph so bad that *any* student can improve it. Reproducing it with triple spacing and wide margins will allow room for revisions on the handout.

### The Model T Ford

You had a good feeling to drive an old model T Ford. When you put up the top the height was seven feet high. The seat where the driver sat was on top of the place where the gas tank was. When the driver wanted to get some gas he had to get out of the front seat and take it out. He would take off the gas tank cap, he would put in a stick to see how much gas he had left. In those days you would not just sit in your car and order the gas through the window you had to get out. These sticks were usually on the floor of the car somewheres, which was usually very messy. Their wasn't to much room under the cussions. The windshield which was in front of the driver was not streamlined it was vertical. The affects of air resistance was not knowed well and anyway the car moved ahead alright so why worry.

If your students would be insulted at this, your adaptation may be less drastic; but I find that some freshmen are so unused to re-writing that the best they can do is a few obvious corrections. Good students are likely to ask whether they may not begin all over on another sheet.

After twenty minutes (or more—this sort of work goes slowly at first), several students read their revised versions and we discuss the improvements. Finally we read the passage in the original essay and call attention to the possibilities realized there.

# Rejuvenating Description

Michael K. Paffard

*Another exercise that can be adapted to various class levels presents a passage that has been drained dry of color and concreteness. Students are asked to expand the desiccate version before ultimate comparison with the original. Mr. Paffard submits exercises from the University of Keele, Staffordshire, England.*

### Author's Comment

This is a type of exercise easily adapted to suit a class of any age, ability, or sex in a secondary school. In essence it consists of the teacher's taking an effective passage from a reputable author and systematically attenuating it; reducing it, in fact, to the low-average standard of the class's performance in composition. The length and structure of sentences are altered; descriptive detail and figures of speech are cut out; overworked and imprecise words are substituted for fresh and precise ones. The example given below should be balanced with other rewriting exercises in which a verbose passage is submitted for rigorous pruning to counter any tendency to overwork figurative language or to fall in-to "adjective stuffing" habits. Passages of narrative, didactic, or rhetorical writing lend themselves equally well to the same basic treatment.

In my experience the exercise is enjoyed: it provides a sense of achievement and an insight into prose styles which have a carry-over effect on subsequent composition and literature work.

*Stage 1*    Issue duplicated passage and instructions to class:

> The very old front of a building came out from behind the trees. It was Oxwell Hall. Oxwell Hall, which was now a farm-house, had once been the home of a family, which was now dead.
>
> The hall was an interesting old building. There was a picture of it in the county history published in 1750 but it was not a very good picture because it did not look very natural.
>
> The building was the sort that is romantic to look at but not very nice to live in, like most of the sort of places that romantic and poetic sort of people imagine they would like to live in but wouldn't really if they tried. The walls were very damp, so was the floor of the larder because things grew between the stones. The outside was very old-looking and worn, especially round the door, and you couldn't tell whether it was the weather or whether it was people that had done it. The iron bars by the windows were almost worn through and the window panes were sort of dull and queer-colored. There was a sundial in the porch but the bit in the middle had come loose so one couldn't tell what time it was supposed to be.

This piece of writing is not strictly incorrect English but it is a dull and ineffective description. Rewrite the passage to bring it to life. You will probably need to expand the original somewhat. Pay attention to:
1    length, structure and arrangement of sentences: test yours aloud to see if they sound right.
2    descriptive detail to make the passage vivid: sparing use of figures of speech, i.e., simile and metaphor, may help.
3    careful choice of words: think about each one you use and be sure there is not a better one to do the job.

*Stage 2*    A composite version of the passage should be worked out on the blackboard, by the teacher, using a selection of the happiest ideas from the class's work. Suggestion, countersuggestion, and criticism will come from the class as the composite version grows.

*Stage 3* Give the class the duplicated passage as originally written (Thomas Hardy, *The Trumpet-Major,* Chapter VI) for comparison with their version. This will provoke lively discussion. Avoid the "This is how you should have done it" sort of approach: their versions may stand the comparison very well and it would be disastrous to think of Hardy as a model. I have never known a class to produce anything comparable to Hardy's touches of ironical humor or fail to be delighted at sharing his sophisticated amusement. They are enlightened rather than offended, too, when they discover that they have been working over a parody of their own style of writing.

> The gray, weather-worn front of a building edged from behind the trees. It was Oxwell Hall, once the seat of a family now extinct, and of late years used as a farmhouse.
>
> The hall was as interesting as mansions in a state of declension usually are, as the excellent county history showed. That popular work in folio contained an old plate dedicated to the last scion of the original owners, from which drawing it appeared that in 1750, the date of publication, the windows were covered with little scratches like black flashes of lightning; that a horn of hard smoke came out of each of the twelve chimneys; that a lady and a lapdog stood on the lawn in a strenuously walking position; and a substantial cloud and nine flying birds of no known species hung over the trees to the northeast.
>
> The rambling and neglected dwelling had all the romantic excellencies and practical drawbacks which such mildewed places share in common with caves, mountains, wildernesses, glens, and other homes of poesy that people of taste wish to live and die in. Mustard and cress could have been raised on the inner plaster of the dewy walls at any height not exceeding three feet from the floor; and mushrooms of the most refined and thin-stemmed kinds grew up through the chinks of the larder paving. As for the outside, Nature, in the ample time that had been given her, had so mingled her filings and effacements with the marks of human wear and tear upon the house, that it was often hard to say in which of the two or if in both, any particular obliteration had its origin. The keenness was gone from the moldings of the doorways, but

whether worn out by the rubbing past of innumerable people's shoulders, and the moving of their heavy furniture, or by Time in a grander and more abstract form, did not appear. The iron stanchions inside the windowpanes were eaten away to the size of wires at the bottom where they entered the stone, the condensed breathings of generations having settled there in pools and rusted them. The panes themselves had either lost their shine altogether or become iridescent as a peacock's tail. In the middle of the porch was a vertical sundial, whose gnomon swayed loosely about when the wind blew, and cast its shadow hither and thither, as much as to say, "Here's your fine model dial; here's any time for any man; I am an old dial; and shiftiness is the best policy."

# Eliminating Wordiness

Laurence Perrine

*Pruning useless verbiage from a doctored paragraph will help students recognize when they themselves are padding or being redundant. Mr. Perrine is professor of English at Southern Methodist University, Dallas, Texas.*

## Author's Comment
This exercise is most effective when it is written on the board and revised by the class in open view of all the students. But as putting it on the board may take too much time, it may have to be duplicated and distributed. The passage is taken from *Selected Papers of Bertrand Russell* (Modern Library), pp. 93-94, but has been amplified by a number of favorite student devices for wordiness.

## Exercise
The following paragraph was taken from an essay by Bertrand Russell. Unfortunately, while being transferred from book to paper, it fell into a puddle and soaked up a great deal of dirty water. Your task is to wring it out. You can easily squeeze out over one hundred words without losing any of the thought. When you have done so, you will find that what is now a muddy muddle is really something you need not be ashamed to wear with your best suit.

It seems that history, in every country, is taught in such a way as to have a tendency to magnify or glorify that country: children can be said to learn to believe that it is their own country which has always been in the right and almost always victorious, that it is their own country which has produced almost all the great men, and that their own country is in all respects quite superior to all other countries. Since these are the sort of beliefs that tend to be flattering, it is obvious that they are quite easily absorbed, and that they are hardly ever dislodged from instinct by the acquisition of later knowledge. As an example of this tendency, let me give this illustration. Take the battle of Waterloo, for example. The facts about the battle of Waterloo are known in great detail and with minute accuracy; but it seems that they as taught in elementary schools will tend to be widely different in England, France, and Germany. The ordinary English boy seems to imagine that the Prussians played hardly any part; on the other hand, the ordinary German boy tends to imagine that Wellington was practically defeated when the day was retrieved by Blucher's gallantry. If the facts were taught accurately and exactly in both of these countries, it is certain that national pride would not be fostered to the same degree or extent, that neither of the two nations would feel quite so certain of obtaining victory in the event that war should come about, and that the willingness to fight would be diminished, at least to some extent.

# Aural Correction of Awkward Sentences

Gerald Siegel

*Some sentences will not reveal to students their difficulties of awkward arrangement, repetitiousness, clumsy movement, monotony, etc. unless heard aloud. Mr. Siegel used this technique at York College of Pennsylvania, York, Pennsylvania.*

One of the most persistent student writing difficulties, the awkward sentence, seems to resist improvement through the usual procedures of writing, marking, and revision. I've been able to improve student handling of awkward sentences through the use of a portable cassette recorder.

The student reads the paper aloud, recording this reading on a cassette. When the cassette is played (a process which can, of course, be repeated as many times as necessary), the awkward sentences often become readily apparent to the student whose ear may catch mistakes the eye has missed. The student can then make changes in these sentences and immediately evaluate the revisions, since the recording provides an objective "instant replay." Use of the recording in this manner also avoids the danger of "reading over" errors, a major weakness of conventional silent proofreading.

# Bibliography

A number of periodicals address themselves to the concerns of the classroom teacher, though most are more specialized than *Exercise Exchange.* In selecting helpful books, I confine my list to material addressed to teachers, recognizing that there are also excellent texts and workbooks primarily aimed at students. One instantly notices, in the material that follows, the primacy of the National Council of Teachers of English in its attention to teaching composition in the classroom.

## Bibliographies

Individual articles on writing are indexed by the *ERIC Clearinghouse on Readings and Communication Skills*, in the *Current Index to Journals in Education* (*CIJE*).

"Selected Bibliography of Research and Writing about the Teaching of Composition, 1973 and 1974," compiled by Richard L. Larson. *College Composition and Communication*, 26 (May 1975), 187-195. (Mr. Larson expressed the hope that this listing of articles with brief abstracts would become an annual event.)

## Books

Clapp, Ouida H., ed. *Classroom Practices in Teaching English 1975-1976: On Righting Writing.* Urbana: NCTE, 1975.

Berger, Allen, and Blanche Hope Smith, eds. *Classroom Practices in Teaching English 1974-1975: Re-Vision.* Urbana: NCTE, 1974.

Geuder, Patricia A., Linda Harvey, Dennis Loyd, and Jack Wages, eds. *They Really Taught Us How to Write.* Urbana: NCTE, 1974.

Ohmann, Richard, and W. B. Coley, eds. *Ideas for English 101: Teaching Writing in College.* Urbana: NCTE, 1975.

Reeves, Ruth, ed. *Ideas for Teaching English: Grades 7-8-9.* Urbana: NCTE, 1966.

## Periodicals and Editorial Addresses

"EJ Teaching Ideas" Department, *English Journal.* Box 112, East Lansing, Michigan 48823. (NCTE)

"EJ Workshop" Department, *English Journal.* (NCTE)

*Exercise Exchange.* Department of English, Old Mill, University of Vermont, Burlington, VT 05401.

*Freshman English News.* Department of English, Texas Christian University, Fort Worth, TX 76129.

*Journal of English Teaching Techniques.* American Language Skills Program and Literature and American Language Program, Southwest Minnesota State College, Marshall, MN 56258.

*Leaflet.* New England Ass'n of Teachers of English, Lee E. Allen, ed. Needham High School, 609 Webster St., Needham, MA 02194.

"Nuts and Bolts" Department, *Media and Methods.* 134 North Thirteenth St., Philadelphia, PA 19107.

*Shop Talk.* English Department, Kansas State University, Manhattan, KS 66502.

"Staffroom Interchange" Department, *College Composition and Communication.* Department of English, Ohio State University, Columbus, OH 43210 (for NCTE).

"Swap Shop" Department, *Learning.* 530 University Ave., Palo Alto, CA 94301.